Acton

£6.95.

KING ALFRED'S COLLEGE
WINCHESTER

To be returned on or before the day marked
below:-

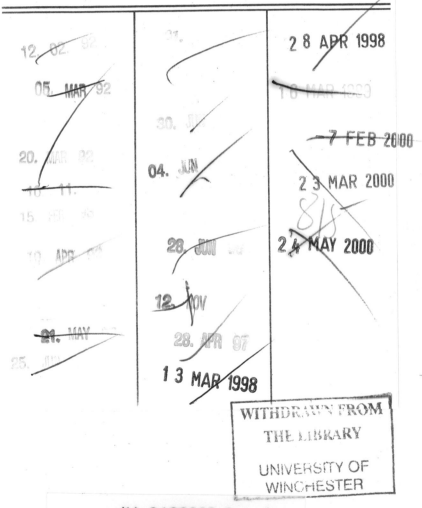

12. 02. 92

05. MAR 92

20. MAR 92

15 FEB

19 APR

21. MAY

25. JUN

31.

30. JUN

04. JUN

28. JUN

12. NOV

28. APR 97

1 3 MAR 1998

2 8 APR 1998

1 6 MAR

7 FEB 2000

2 3 MAR 2000

2 4 MAY 2000

Historians on Historians

Hugh Tulloch on **Acton**
Roy Porter on **Gibbon**
Owen Dudley Edwards on **Macaulay**

Forthcoming titles

John Gould on **Herodotus**
Nicholas Phillipson on **Hume**
Linda Colley on **Namier**
David Cannadine on **Trevelyan**

Hugh Tulloch

Acton

St. Martin's Press
New York

Printed in Great Britain

ISBN 0–312–02726–5

Library of Congress Cataloging-in-Publication Data

Tulloch, Hugh.
   Acton/Hugh Tulloch.
      p.   cm.—(Historians on historians)
   Bibliography: p.
   Includes index.
   ISBN 0-312-02726-5
   1. Acton, John Emerich Edward Dalberg Acton, Baron, 1834–1902.
   2. Historians—Great Britain—Biography. I. Title. II. Series.
D15.A25T85 1988
907′.2024—dc19
[B]   88-27593 CIP

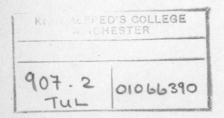

Contents

Acknowledgements

A study based mainly on secondary reading is uncommonly dependent on previous researchers in the field and I am heavily indebted to their quarrying, as my Bibliography and Notes reveal. The greatest pleasure in writing a book lies in formally thanking friends and colleagues who helped and assisted at every stage. My gratitude is extended to virtually every member of my department who helped in those many areas where I was unusually ignorant. Gratitude, too, towards my bemused first-year students who suffered and endured. My special thanks go to Gordon Blair, Hugh Brogan and Allegra Huston who kindly read the typescript, to Norman Livingston, Irena Grugulis, the Hon. Mrs Douglas Woodruff, herself an Acton, Dr Owen, custodian of the Acton papers in the Cambridge University library, Anita Hathway who typed at inconvenient times, and to Juliet Gardner – an editor of the sort most authors, unhappily, only dream of having – for her sympathy and encouragement.

Chronology

1880–85   Adviser to Gladstone's second ministry and advocate of Irish home rule

1889   Review of James Bryce's *American Commonwealth*

1892–95   Lord in Waiting to Queen Victoria

1895   Appointed Regius Professor of Modern History at Cambridge. Delivers lectures on modern history and the French revolution. Editor of *Cambridge Modern History*

1902   Death at Tegernsee

1904   Acton–Mary Gladstone correspondence published

1906   Cardinal Gasquet edits Acton–Simpson correspondence

1931   Herbert Butterfield's *Whig Interpretation of History*

1952   Gertrude Himmelfarb's *Lord Acton*. First full biography

1 The Reputation

Every schoolboy knows two things and two things only about Lord Acton: that he wrote nothing, and that he uttered the famous dictum 'Power tends to corrupt and absolute power corrupts absolutely.' Like the schoolboy most historians, who should know better, continue to believe the former and misquote the latter. Yet even those readers who manage to jump these initial hurdles are usually discouraged from proceeding when beset by a multitude of further offputting problems and paradoxes. They discover, for example, that Acton was a liberal Catholic in the age of the reactionary Pius IX and Cardinal Manning; that he introduced scientific German methods into England yet claimed, at the same time, to write definitive history and went in for passing final judgements on the great and good of the past. This not only smacked of the simplicities of 1066 *And All That*, of Bad King John and Good Queen Bess, but also, in its impossible attempt to emancipate the historian from the present and deny historical relativism, committed two of the greatest sins against orthodoxy. We all know that historians are inside history and not outside it, that the past is different from the present, and that it is very foolish and misguided to pretend otherwise.

Perhaps it was because he persisted, even gloried, in his perversity to the very end that the profession have at times harried him with a ferocity unusual even by their standards, unaware that in hanging Acton for being a hanging judge they might themselves be behaving in a self-contradictory fashion. Yet judge they have, and even when favourably they have usually hedged round their appreciation with qualifications. Edward Norman, for example, discovered an 'elliptical knowledge', and David Ogg 'a real though occluded greatness'; William McNeill, the American historian, spoke of 'learned trifles'; H.A.L.Fisher conceded more but also suggested that Acton required 'a special line of defence'. If all of this seems like damning with faint praise no such reservations have hindered the brutal frankness of two of our most distinguished living historians. The first, Geoffrey Elton, is quite happy to consign Acton to 'that honourable oblivion which that unproductive monument really deserves'. Acton was an amateur who had never served his apprenticeship in the PRO. Worse still was Acton's untidy habit of uncovering a mass of fresh historical problems and leaving the humbler professional like himself to come along afterwards and clean up the mess. To waste precious hours attempting to decipher him, as Herbert Butterfield did, was to incur a suspicion of unsoundness, and Elton is proud to record that as a member of the Cambridge History faculty he managed to fix a maximum quota of three research students losing themselves in the maze of Acton's manuscripts at any one time. The second, A.J.P.Taylor, is witheringly dismissive: Acton was 'one of the great frauds of Christendom'.[1] I am not sure what Taylor means by this and perhaps Acton, who had devoted his life to the very task of exposing the sources of fraud and deceit in Christendom, might have been amused by such an attack and from such a quarter. But these and similar dismissals will force anyone with the temerity to embark on yet another brief study to ask himself if anything can be salvaged and, if it can, whether it would be worth the trouble.

In one sense Acton unwittingly aided and abetted his detractors by exemplifying a cosmopolitan exoticism which could only alienate the stolid insular virtues of the English historical profession. He was Catholic, he was aristocratic and he was in part foreign. Separately each of these characteristics would have been a drawback; combined they were unforgivable. Catholicism was rather unEnglish, distasteful to a milder latitudinarian tradition and, with its whiff of Jesuitical sophistry and curial intrigue, obscurantist and unscientific. As an aristocrat Acton could hardly be expected to write anything but élitist history, and an élite history of a peculiarly limited and questionable sort, obsessed as it was with court intrigues and Cabinet gossip, lurid melodrama and sinister secrets. Acton would attempt to disentangle the intricate web spun round the Casket Letters, probe the mystery surrounding Marie Antoinette's diamonds, retrace the fortunes of a forgotten, illegitimate son of Charles II and measure the distance of Louis XVI's flight to Varennes. He reads at times like a detective story, concerning himself with whether Pope Alexander VI died a natural death or succumbed instead to verdigris in the saucepan or to toadstools planted among the mushrooms. His Bavarian connections and German training hinted at interminable footnotes, obscure references, leaden prose and Teutonic pedantry or, worse still, a damaging preoccupation with grandiose Hegelian concepts, of universal history and a dreary *Weltanschauung* antipathetic to a more robust but modest homegrown empiricism. Acton made matters worse by chastising the English for their parochial philistinism, their traditional insistence that history was something one wrote rather than thought about: 'What is mind? No matter. What is matter? Never mind.'[2] At times his own writing seemed drained of actual life, disembodied, intensely cerebral, in which those reliable and reassuring props – states, frontiers, wars, treaties, dates of reigns – seemed to dissolve under his rarefied pen to be replaced by tenuous and uncertain trends and the pedigree of ideas which seemed to lead back in infinite regression to obscure books from which he would pluck out a decisive phrase here or a seminal sentence there. There was little that was solid, substantial, nutritive, and too often the weary pursuit of an idea to its source led not to a spring but to the disappearance of water in a waste of sand. He concentrated too exclusively upon the idea that provoked the action and neglected the vital consequent action itself; he would emphasize the Abbe Siéyès' *Qu'est-ce que le Tiers-État?* at the expense of the storming of the Bastille. At its worst this degenerated into mere list-making, his mind, as Fisher put it, being constituted in bibliographies. The 100

3

Best Books drawn up for the hapless Mary Gladstone (the prime minister's daughter, later Mrs Drew) contained mainly German authors, the vast majority unknown to the most erudite Englishman.

Was Acton being deliberately obscure, playing cat and mouse to shore up a spurious reputation? He could be provokingly oblique at times. What, for example, was one to make of 'the unguarded sentence in *The Wealth of Nations* which gave to the Provençal priest the fulcrum to overturn the monarchy of Louis XVI'? Was the fact that Acton knew what the reader might not, that the sentence referred to Adam Smith's theory of labour as source of wealth and that the priest is Siéyès, merely evidence of intellectual arrogance, of showing off? Another stratagem was to flatten opposition from the outset by mustering all his multilingual skill into a first disabling paragraph. Thus in his review of James Bryce's *American Commonwealth*, a book he found distressingly factual, being almost wholly concerned with bosses and booms, hoodlums and mugwumps, he launches his criticism by quoting variously in partly unattributed Latin, German and French. Similarly, he made few concessions to the students who attended his course of lectures on modern European history at Cambridge in the 1890s. The *Saturday Review* complained of his 'Batavian splutterings', and Oscar Browning, a historian of a more mundane nature, had to run a concurrent series of lectures to explain and flesh out the Professor's more gnomic utterances.[3]

All this massive erudition might be magnificent, but was it history? Those colleagues who remained unconvinced, prolific writers whatever the quality of their work, had to hand the most powerful weapon of retaliation of all – the fellow hadn't written a thing. It was surely understandable that the gentle Mandell Creighton, harassed almost beyond endurance by Acton (when asked by Creighton to review his own *History of the Papacy* in the *English Historical Review* which he edited, Acton had replied with an intemperate critique), should take the opportunity to point out, when his back was

4

pinned against the wall, that the 'mere fact that you [Acton] have not fallen into the vulgar error of writing a book gives you an additional claim to attention'.[4] *Touché*, is the reader's instant response at this juncture of the Acton–Creighton correspondence. Many years later Sir Charles Oman, precisely one of that order of historians who chose to write a good deal more than his public chose to read, visited the dead historian's library at Aldenham and observed the sheets spread over the furniture, the coating of dust covering each copy of the huge 60,000-volume library, each book read and annotated and crammed full of thin slips of paper, and was moved to reflect upon the vanity of human life and learning. The moral was obvious: publish or be damned. There were, of course, Acton's last productive Cambridge years given over to editing the *Cambridge Modern History*. But then again Acton contributed nothing to it, not even an introduction (Creighton filled the gap) and as its twelve-volume unreadability became the despair of generations of students, its sinking reputation inexorably carried Acton along with it. It became, as Hugh Trevor-Roper pointed out, his grim tombstone.

There was a vague awareness that he had written pieces of 'hack journalism' – the phrase is J.P. Kenyon's – and long-forgotten polemics, but these usually turned out on inspection to be tiresomely shrill and sterile in their negativism. The reader could easily weary of the extravagant hyperbole and repeated condemnations from which no one seemed to escape. This was not history but a quirky neurotic obsession which mistakenly grafted ethics on to history. Mary Gladstone recorded an evening spent with Acton at his home at Tegernsee in Bavaria, in September 1879: 'H [Herbert her brother] and I sat up to 1. Lord Acton lectured us on intolerance.' Every reader of Acton has undergone a similar sinking experience and wished like Mary that just once in a while he would stop indulging his priggish rectitude; or to lecture him for a change: 'There is in some quarter a general idea that you do nothing but criticize with folded hands – that you are always negative – that nobody knows anything at all about your real opinions – that you continually pull down and tear to pieces, without raising up or edifying.' Acton, who usually replied with mocking irony, that defensive weapon of the insecure, occasionally admitted he could be 'obstructive', adopt 'a too perpetual note of interrogation', could, in a word, be a 'bore'.[5]

What else remained? There were the famous notes, the raw materials of history, quotations and reflections written on separate record cards to be sifted and resifted, shaken like a kaleidoscope to reveal a new pattern each time as more cards were added and a fesh reassessment begun. But if these were the real legacy they constituted a formidable obstacle to genuine understanding. For a historian he was careless about dating, of attributing source or provenance; he was given to intellectual somersaults – consistency, he maintained, was puerile – and it was only too easy for the confused researcher lost in the labyrinth to shuffle the cards and come up with violently contradictory statements. More disarmingly the researcher reconstructing Acton's intellectual development could never be sure he was actually reading Acton; he might as easily be reading Acton's unattributed record of conversations with Döllinger, his mentor, or indeed anyone else Acton had talked to or read. The beautiful clear handwriting disguised fiendishly compressed thoughts, cramped unpunctuated hieroglyphics, which were as difficult to decipher as any delphic utterance. Here as elsewhere Acton actively collaborated with those who wished to bury him.

But his professional colleagues had not always wished to do so, and perhaps Acton's excessively high reputation among his contemporaries contributed inevitably to the subsequent slump in his stock. During his lifetime he was forced into the role of high priest, liberal guru, a scholar seemingly crushed into pregnant silence by an insupportable erudition and wisdom. This elevated pigeon-holing was to do him no good at all as a politician among the strictly political class of men like Lord Spencer and Sir William Harcourt; and at Hawarden, when he wished only to play cards with the children, he was made instead to listen (he speaks of 'a dread-ful hour' and 'a hard trial') while Gladstone held forth interminably on the vexed question of Homeric authorship. His contemporaries chose to stuff him while he was still alive, while those fortunate enough to hear him outline his projected *History of Freedom* underwent what can only be described as a pentecostal experience. This privilege was extended to Mary and Herbert Gladstone one evening in Venice in September 1879 as they strolled through the Piazza San Marco: 'It is extraordinary the way he tingles with it to his fingers' ends and yet can sit patient and quiet over wife and children and wait and wait another year before he writes it.' On another occasion the revelation was vouchsafed to James Bryce, the Liberal politician. Acton spoke but six or seven minutes late at night in his library at Cannes, but he spoke like a man inspired, a visionary, viewing the course of history as from a mountain summit, when all at once – 'It was as if the whole landscape of history had been suddenly lit up by a burst of sunlight.'[6] Bryce was to cherish this memory for the remainder of his life.

This was a hard act to follow, and necessarily the remembrance of such epiphanies grew scarcer as those who had enjoyed personal contact in turn passed away. Even some contemporaries remained immune to the Actonian magic. One, from a surprising quarter, was never taken in for a minute. Henry James, who could match Acton in his understanding of the wayward heart if not in learning, was an American outsider who enjoyed all the privileges of an insider, and remained resolutely unimpressed. 'Acton was an intellectual dilettante, wallowing in curious intellectual luxury. An interesting figure, of course, from his social station and his cosmopolitanism ... But he must have been stupid at bottom. There must have been a great fund of stupidity in anyone who could write such long letters to Mary Gladstone.' This appraisal is even more surprising because the novelist was a Liberal supporter; and he, of all people, accused Acton of 'verbal juggling' and of being remote 'from the realities of practical life'.[7]

No one could accuse the younger generation of Cambridge historians – Frederic Maitland, G.M.Trevelyan, G.P.Gooch – of being remote, and when Acton took up residence in Trinity College in 1895, the sacred flame was kept alight and passed on from master to disciples. Maitland's veneration is especially interesting because his own history, concentrating on the minute inspection of legal documents to illuminate medieval English life, was as far removed from that of the Regius Professor's as it was possible to be. Yet, having intended to scoff, Maitland's letters show a rapid reversion to prayer. There is a growing respect for Acton's renovation of the Cambridge History faculty, for the new breadth and vision he brought after the staleness of Seeley, for his professor's 'Napoleonic' grasp of history (he felt certain that Acton could have written all twelve volumes of the *CMH* himself) and his devotion to hunting out the little fact that makes all the difference.[8] Gooch and Trevelyan concentrated on those aspects of Acton which made most sense to them, the 'apostle of liberty', and carried that light with them into a darker century. Many new readers came to marvel at Acton's prescience and wisdom. He alone seemed to have foreseen the coming nightmare of totalitarian tyranny, dissected the morbid pathology of power, had foreknowledge of the evil consequences of nationalism: rampant militarism, the crushing of the individual conscience and the oppression of spiritual conformity. His youthful essay on 'Nationality' alone ensured his survival. Employed as high-brow propaganda against the Third Reich it was dusted down once more as a Cold War weapon aimed at the heart of Communist tyranny. To 'liberal apostle' was added the more enduring title of 'prophet of the twentieth century'.

Suddenly Acton was resurrected and refurbished anew to combat a host of post-war demons. There were a few dissenting voices; Herman Finer questioned the role of Acton as prophet of the new order, and E.D.Watt dismissed his writings on liberty as mere mystical incantation. But far more influential and lasting were the voices of a powerful group of intellectual *émigrés* – Friedrich von Hayek, Karl Popper, Isaiah Berlin – who discerned two basic historical modes of thinking. The first, traced back to Plato and fortified by Hegel and Marx, was the all-encompassing and enslaving utopian ideal; the other, critical, limited, humane, constructive, was the tradition of Erasmus and Montaigne, Montesquieu, Hume, Adam Smith and Tocqueville, with Acton as one of its latest and fullest flowerings. In 1944, the year of his *Road to Serfdom*, Hayek proposed a type of cerebral Morgenthau plan, with the setting up of groups of Acton Societies throughout Germany, to remove the stain of Nazism and turn bad Germans into good. For Acton was the type of German 'with whom no Englishman need feel reluctant to shake hands', and his advocacy of pluralism in 'Nationality' was the chosen weapon by which to slay Hitler and Stalin, Beatrice Webb and Harold Laski, and all those mischievous visionaries who desired the social engineering and planned economy of the welfare state. The current, magnificent republication of Acton's selected writings comes to us by courtesy of Liberty Fund, Inc., while the most recent biography of Acton, by Robert Schuettinger, is funded by the right-wing American Heritage foundation and is dedicated to Hayek. Its author quotes with approval Acton's opposition to the increased state powers provided under the poor-law administration in 1862, but omits to quote any of the historian's maturer, perilously socialist, reflections.[9]

But Acton's renaissance owed even more to a post-war thirst for moral order. Acton was a good German because he would not have attempted to explain Hitler away. Popper's *The Open Society and Its Enemies* was specifically aimed at destroying an insidious moral relativism which sapped the life of reason. History with values may be whig, but it was humane: fact and evaluation were inextricably mixed and history could be a moral fable by which to combat what Hayek considered the profound amorality which Maynard Keynes carried with him from Bloomsbury into economics, much as it could be used against the totalitarian demotion of history to the Department of Propaganda. In the night of dissolving values and universal scepticism, Acton's plea that the historian's aim was 'to develop and perfect and arm conscience' was a potent antidote.[10]

Acton's reputation as a historian fared less well. In an increasingly secular century, Acton's Catholicism remained a problem: to John Morley, H.A.L.Fisher, G.P.Gooch, and to Lytton Strachey when in 1918 he came indiscriminately to blow up nineteenth-century faith. Added to the revengeful parricide of Bloomsbury, the author of *Eminent Victorians* contributed a more personal rationalism, a debunking Voltairian spirit which conceived of the nineteenth century as an inexplicable and unforgivable lapse in taste from high eighteenth-century enlightenment back into medieval mysticism and religious cant. Strachey had no trouble disposing of the spiritual humbug of Manning and other predatory princes of the Church who called upon God to advance their careers, but Acton was a man of genuine learning and enlightened principles, so that his adherence to an obscurantist Church was simply incomprehensible. How could 'that lifelong enthusiast for liberty, that almost hysterical reviler of priesthood and persecution, [trail]... his learning so discrepantly along the dusty Roman way'?[11] How could Acton strain at the gnat of infallibility yet swallow the camel of the faith? Strachey could only conclude that learning and judgement had not been granted him in equal proportion.

Religious faith was also a problem to E.H.Carr and other historians trained in the hard school of *Realpolitik*, to whom Acton increasingly became not the first of the twentieth-century realists but rather the apotheosis of Victorian delusions. Optimism had perished in August 1914. Like Fisher and Arnold Toynbee, Acton spoke out from 'the positive belief, the clear-eyed self-confidence, of the later Victorian age' and, speaking from a quite different universal order, could hold no relevance for the disenchanted twentieth-century predicament. Indeed, having survived and recorded the Russian

Revolution and the twenty-year crisis, having shared the political world with Mussolini and Franco, Hitler and Stalin, Carr managed to convince himself that original sin was the exclusive discovery of post-1914 historians. Victorian optimism was based on the even more deplorable fallacy of inevitable progress which assumed that ultimately God made up in righteousness whatever the true cause lacked in big battalions to guarantee eventual victory. At least the neo-determinism of Marx had no need to introduce a joker into the pack, a convenient *deus ex machina*, who would explain everything, for in explaining everything it failed to explain anything at all. To ascribe the cause of the First World War or of the Russian Revolution to God did not get the historian very far. Yet here was Acton, wedged between J.R.Seeley, who looked upon history as a training school for imperial statesmanship, and J.B.Bury who believed history was a pure science, invoking God in his inaugural lecture at Cambridge as supreme historian and guarantor of liberal destiny: that 'the action of Christ who is risen on mankind whom he redeemed fails not, but increases; that the wisdom of divine rule appears not in the perfection but in the improvement of the world; and that achieved liberty is the one ethical result that rests on the converging and combined conditions of advancing civilization'.[12] Having rescued history from the grip of scholasticism it seemed perverse to return it once more in 1895 to theology in the shape of providence.

It might have been assumed that Christian historians such as David Knowles and Herbert Butterfield would find themselves more in sympathy with Acton. On the contrary, not only did they make no attempt at rehabilitation, but Butterfield specifically destroyed what remained of his reputation in a single blow. Both Butterfield and Knowles knew that God was indubitably there; he was not an absentee who, once having set the world in motion, left frail humanity to its own muddled devices to make do as best it could. Rather the world and the world's history rested in the hollow of God's hand. Yet it was equally clear from the most cursory reflection on history that God was not around much of the time. Acton's first impudence lay in his insistence on bringing God back on to centre stage, his second was to charge the historians to discern God's role in the temporal world, and his third, compounding his errors, was in blasphemously taking on God's mantle as judge of the quick and the dead. Butterfield was unable to discern the hand of God directly in profane history. Providential history was God's history. The more mundane task of the 'technical' historian was simply to bear witness, not to prosecute, defend or judge. Acton's attempts to discern the divine economy were not only an illicit usurpation but also a form of self-aggrandizement. It was not the historian's job to meddle in theology, to

> take upon's the mystery of things,
> As if we were God's spies.

Not only was it a profanation to presume to interpret God's unknowable will, it was also unChristian. Charged with surveying the unending tragic conflict of earthly existence, both historian and Christian should be humbled in their vocation. Confronted by the implacability of evil, it was manifestly wrong to cast the first stone, to judge lest you yourself be judged, for each judgement was a self-judgement. The contemplation of history should rather evoke the Christian virtues of charity, sympathy and compassion. Indeed Butterfield's own studies finally left him feeling saddened and sorry for just about everyone and, in print at least, exhibiting a humility that bordered on self-abasement. If history was a harlot then the historian was a hireling, a drudge of all the drudges. Finally, moral indignation was not only damaging to the soul but made for poor history; to judge was a futile indulgence which precluded full historical understanding; it closed rather than opened doors. And because moral judgements were a loophole for every abuse in historical study, and because Butterfield considered the compulsion to judge the past in terms of the present to be the very essence of whiggism, he concluded that 'in Lord Acton, the whig historian reached his highest consciousness'.[13]

The irony is that Butterfield's initial, damning reassessment gave way to a growing admiration after the publication of his seminal *Whig Interpretation of History* in 1931. He now spoke of the wonderful jewel this particular toad had encased in its forehead. But the damage was done; Butterfield's own reputation was built upon the ruin of Acton's, who was thereafter labelled and dismissed as 'whig'; the jewel was forgotten and only the toad remembered. So Denis Brogan, who admitted, disconcertingly, that he had read little Acton and did not like what little he had read, disposed of him along with Macaulay as naive, innocent and arch-whig. Hugh Trevor-Roper, in an otherwise sensible introduction to Acton's lectures on modern history, also labelled him as an aristocratic English whig.[14]

Nor were other professional fads and fashions calculated to resurrect or enhance Acton's fallen status. At Manchester University, and in exile from a dismembered eastern Europe, Lewis Namier set about reimagining an eighteenth-century world of extraordinary stability which implicitly challenged the pernicious intrusion of Wilsonian idealism into post-war Europe. He conjured up a British political system in which factions replaced parties, jobbery and patronage disruptive principles, in which the momentous birth of American republicanism barely entered into the complex calculations of Parliament where men pursued office and not ideologies. This 'Namierization' of history – a history emptied of ideas and ideals – exerted a seminal influence not least at Cambridge where the History faculty contrived to turn its one-time Regius professor into a dodo. To the hard-nosed conservative school that emerged he was useful only as an easy target by which to nail the 'liberal myth' which that school felt had penetrated and softened academia.[15] Maurice Cowling for one intended Acton as a sacrificial victim before turning instead to destroy John Stuart Mill, perhaps realizing in time that the youthful Acton had reaped all the ripe wisdom to be gained from

Burkean *praxis* before going on to reject it as wholly inadequate in his maturity. One was on much clearer ground when it became a straight contrast of Mill versus Lord Salisbury. Those historians of power who measured achievement by results, who found room for Thomas Cromwell and stripped away the Catholic hagiography surrounding Thomas More to reveal the persecutor, were unlikely to succumb to the Actonian stress on the sovereign conscience. The purveyors of high politics converted conscience into a gambit, a stratagem adopted by powerful men seeking greater personal and party power in the corridors of Westminster. Acton's distinction of 'conscience' and 'power' was meaningless to them.

Neither was the increased reputation of social history a congenial atmosphere for disinterested re-evaluation. Acton's loathing of materialism either in the shape of Buckle's statistical averages or Marx's clash of classes, his distaste for anything which detracted from the great moral drama of individual free will in history, would have left him more sympathetic even to godless French existentialism than to the *longue durée* of Braudel and the Annales school which was more successful in infiltrating British universities. The profoundly conservative undertow of social history, with its emphasis on the sluggish predetermined pull of soil, climate and harvest and the almost equally prohibiting and retarding human agencies of prices and populations, found no place for Acton's superficial concern with ephemeral political *événements*. A historical world in which the character of the Mediterranean basin was more striking than that of Philip II was not one that Acton would have recognized. The growing concern to rediscover the lost past of the inarticulate and the dispossessed revealed a world dominated by dire material necessity in which ideas became an epicurean luxury: the stress was on grub before ethics. Thus, in their distinct approaches, both high and low politics tended to diminish the role of ideas in history.

Immediately following his death various factions laid exclusive claim to Acton's soul. In 1904 Herbert Paul's edition of the Acton–Mary Gladstone correspondence revealed a Liberal radical dallying with socialist principles. In response the second Lord Acton charged Cardinal Gasquet, a scholar so notoriously inaccurate that he was given to referring to Gibbon's *Rise and Fall of the Roman Empire*, to reaffirm his father's loyal Catholicism. The consequent volume of the Acton–Simpson correspondence, published in 1906, combined the faults of slovenly editorship with a more insidious policy of bowdlerization. Negatives suddenly sprouted where none had existed before, so that Acton now held the view that St Augustine was *not* a Jansenist; Pius IV was no longer an 'ass', merely 'no good'; the splendid childishness of 'Old Nogs' was replaced by the more respectful 'Newman'.[16] Thereafter Acton continued to receive the passing attention of prejudice rooted in ignorance, variously damned without being read, treated almost exclusively as a gilded aristocrat of the *ancien régime*, portrayed as a loyal son of Holy Mother Church, reprinted as propaganda for a neo-conservative orthodoxy or used as a means of spiking a 'liberal myth'. Happily, at the same time, a solid body of disinterested scholarship has grown to supplement the earlier labours of Herbert Paul and Figgis and Laurence and provide ample material for a fresh appraisal based on Acton's own notes, writings and correspondence.

I am not here attempting an apology or a rehabilitation. I hope, in part at least, that this brief study is an appreciation: an appreciation of the intellectual excitement derived from reading Acton as well as an awareness of the dangers involved; the conviction that there exists a store of wisdom, that he addressed himself persistently and obsessively to matters of vital historical importance and revealed again and again that historiography, far from being otiose and parasitic, was central to the historian's task. More than any other he propounded the ideal aims of that vocation while simultaneously illustrating the impossibility of attaining such an ideal. Both aspects can be equally illuminating, for Acton fell into almost every pitfall he warned us about. He was deeply flawed as man and historian; he could write like an angel, yet what he wrote could lapse from one extreme into another without once deviating into sensible moderation. It was the denial that he had written anything at all, persistently levelled by reputable historians who had lazily picked it up at second hand, that first prompted me to write. Having started, I found my response to Acton wavering inconsistently between admiration and dislike and, if muddled, this equivocation had the advantage at least of avoiding a stark and partial portrait, of depicting him neither as shaman nor fraud, but as a historian who was all too accessibly human. Acton would have hated above everything to be posthumously hitched to any particular cause, and this I have tried to avoid. For I do not believe that he was whig or naive, innocent or optimistic, and in hoping to rescue him from the partial understanding of his detractors I have had to treat him in a profoundly unActonian way. He always insisted that the historian must disappear entirely from his history: I am unable to separate the two. Despite his many disavowals, the man and the historian were not distinct, nor were his historical writings separate from his personal history. At each juncture of his life, as combative Catholic, as arch-enemy of ultramontanism, as Gladstonian Liberal, the pressures of his current preoccupations subtly intrude, moulding and distorting his vision. I hope that a study of the historian enmeshed in his time will contribute towards a clearer and more balanced understanding.

2 The Catholic

John Emerich Edward Dalberg Acton was born in Naples
on 10 January 1834, the descendant of a cadet branch of
'that ancient and loyal family of Shropshire Baronets' with
whom Edward Gibbon was proud to claim connections. It
was his great-grandfather, Edward Acton, who rushed from
his medical studies in Paris to attend Gibbon's father when
he became dangerously ill in Besançon. Attending to the re-
covery of his patient the physician was in turn infected by
the malady of love, married, and settled in that town where
the historian's grandfather, John Acton, was born in 1736.
Twenty-six years later Gibbon met his kinsman on his travels;
he records in his *Journal* having consumed an excessive
amount of wine in his company, and judged him to be 'a
very pretty sensible young man'.[1] In 1791 the senior branch
died out and Sir John succeeded to the title and estates of
Aldenham, but in the meantime the ambitious young adven-
turer had gone off to Italy in search of his fortune and had
risen to the rank of Chief Minister under Ferdinand and Maria
Carolina of the Two Sicilies. It was gossiped abroad that Sir
John's advancement at the Neapolitan court was owing to
the Queen having taken him for a lover, but it is far more
likely that his precarious hold on power was the result of
that shrewdness and sense noted by Gibbon. Nevertheless
it was a strange and exotic ancestry for the austere historian.
Monsieur de Bérenger, the French Chargé d'Affaires, reported
that 'The tone of brazen familiarity, indecency and licentious-
ness prevailing at this Court is inconceivable,' and when in
1806 the French invaded the kingdom and forced the court
to flee to Palermo, Sir John instigated a reign of terror to
counter the spread of revolution in Sicily.[2] This was later

to prove a source of deep embarrassment to the historian, especially when his friendship with Gladstone ripened, for it was Gladstone who in 1850 exposed the appalling conditions in the prisons of the kingdom and the general contempt for civil liberties expressed by King Bomba. Acton always refused to accept the income from his Neapolitan estates.

To the great surprise of the court Sir John announced his engagement to a thirteen-year-old niece at the age of sixty-four, and before his death in 1811 his young wife gave birth to three children. The second son, Charles Januarius (1803–47), entered the Church and was appointed a cardinal by Gregory XVI as a reward for his strenuous efforts on behalf of the hierarchy. The eldest son, Richard, added considerably to the family fortune by marrying Marie Pelline de Dalberg, heiress of one of the most ancient and illustrious families of the Holy Roman Empire who brought as her dowry large hereditary estates in the Rhineland. Sir Richard died prematurely in Paris in 1837, three years after the birth of his only son, and in 1840 Acton's widowed mother married Lord Leveson Gower, later the second Earl Granville, a leading whig aristocrat related to the Dukes of Devonshire and Sutherland. Thus, throughout his life, Acton moved with ease, not just between the family houses in London, Aldenham, Paris, Herrnsheim and Naples, but through the drawing rooms of the ruling families of half Europe. He became a fluent conversationalist in English, French, German and Italian.

But his was above all a profoundly Catholic and Continental inheritance. The earlier chance securing of the Shropshire estates, his mother's later remarriage, were far less influential in shaping and moulding the young historian. Those English traditions of latitudinarianism, of public service as an extension of landlord husbandry, the settled seasonal ritual of country-house parties and hunting – Acton was an appalling shot – were alien to a child steeped from birth in a stifling Continental clericalism so different from his stepfather's easy progress from Eton to Christ Church to high political office. It was one of the stipulations laid down by his devout mother on her marriage to the Anglican lord that her son continue to be educated in the Roman faith. At the age of five he began his studies under Dupanloup, his mother's confessor and spiritual adviser. Between 1843 and 1848 he was boarded at Oscott, 'that great engine employed in England's conversion and regeneration' as its head, Nicholas Wiseman, later Cardinal and first Archbishop of Westminster, called it. After a brief period in Edinburgh under a private tutor he applied in 1850 for admission to Cambridge: 'At three colleges I applied ... and, as things then were, I was refused by all.'[3] But this refusal was to result in the most formative decision of his life, for he gained permission from his stepfather to travel instead to Munich to study privately under the famous Catholic theologian, Ignaz von Döllinger. This and his obedience to his mother's dying wish that he marry her Bavarian cousin, Countess Marie von Arco-Valley, served to strengthen further his close links with southern Germany and with Catholicism. Lord Granville also remarried and continued to believe that 'Johnny' was as moderate in his Catholicism as in his Liberalism. But then Granville never really understood his extraordinary stepson; the gulf separating them was too wide, and there are hints, nothing more, of psychological trauma suffered by the young Acton on his beloved mother's remarriage. What she gave him was something he never lost: a simple piety which was to sustain him spiritually throughout his life.

From childhood onwards he held fast to the basic tenets of his Christian faith; the existence of God, the immortality of the soul, the punishment of sin. To Lord Mountstuart Grant Duff he confessed that he was never conscious of ever having entertained the slightest shadow of a doubt about fundamental Church dogma. Cardinal Newman, who knew him well and had borne many trials on his behalf, could assert with perfect truth that Acton had 'ever been a religious, well-conducted, conscientious Catholic from a boy'. Acton believed that faith was an unfathomable mystery unreachable by reason alone; that revelation revealed an inexhaustible fund of truth, and that it required the submission of the intellect and the suspension of critical faculties to attain it. 'If all ... truths could be ascertained,' he wrote, 'no revelation would be needed. If reason could demonstrate all truths, there would be no room for faith. As long as mysteries remain in religion, there are limits set to reason; there is a domain of imperative authority.' To those to whom it was granted faith was an ineffable benediction, an ever-present awareness of the trans-cendental, a bestowal of grace granted to the pure in heart. 'I think,' he wrote to Mary Gladstone, 'that faith implies sin-cerity, that it is a gift that does not dwell in dishonest minds.'[4] It was during the greatest personal crisis of his life, when threatened by excommunication, that he realized that he could not bear to contemplate existence outside a Church whose sacrament was dearer to him than life itself.

His private expressions of faith read rather mawkishly today. When Archbishop Darboy was executed by the Communards in 1871, he wrote to his wife insisting that the children pray daily for the soul of the good Archbishop who loved papa; in his short *History of England*, written for the edification of his children, he wrote of Thomas More's death as the happiest that God could give, 'death for the Catholic faith'; at his daughter's deathbed his last words to her were 'Be glad, my child, you will soon be with Jesus Christ.'[5] It was because he was a true believer that he could discern the hand of God despite the apostasy of heroes, the weakness of rulers, the error of doctors or the death of a much loved child. Because he distinguished between the visible and the invisible Church, the outward shell of variable opinion and the inward core of irreversible dogma, he could severely chas-tise authority yet believe himself a good Catholic. Born within the fold of the Church, he never suffered the agonizing doubts of Newman or Manning who, on conversion, were less critical of their faith precisely because it constituted their ultimate refuge from too much questioning. Acton's unshakeable certitude set no limits to questioning.

But the Church was not only the receptacle of divine revela-tion, it was also a historical institution dedicated to creating and preserving the preconditions of liberty under which the truth of God could alone be attained. In his notes Acton copied out the definition of conscience which he found in the writings of Vinet, a Swiss Protestant theologian: 'Conscience is not ourselves; it is against us; therefore it is something other than ourselves. But if it is other than ourselves, what can it be but God?' God had planted conscience in each man, and granted him the free will to choose between good and evil. This conscience was not, as Gladstone believed, infallible, for Acton did not have sufficient faith in the promptings of human virtue. Individual conscience required the assistance of divine guidance to create the desired end of liberty, but because liberty to choose was itself 'so holy a thing ... God was forced to permit evil, that it might exist'.[6] This God-given freedom had been granted in order not that we may do as we like, but that we be given the choice of doing what we ought, to extract good, continuously and unremittingly, from evil. Creating a dualism within each human soul, God had also created a dualism on earth by creating a Church which sustained a spiritual order immune from the temporal sphere. Christ's admonition that each should render unto Caesar those things that were Caesar's, and unto God those things which were God's, established a visible Church whose duty it was to protect the sovereignty of conscience.

Acton's comment to Mary Gladstone in 1881, that he had never had any contemporaries, has been quoted endlessly to emphasize his alienation from the Victorian world around him, but quoted in context it is clear that Acton intended this quite literally.

> Being refused at Cambridge, and driven to foreign universities, I never had any contemporaries, but spent years in looking for men wise enough to solve the problems which puzzled me, not in religion and politics so much as along the wavy line between the two. So I was always associated with men a generation older than myself, most of whom died early – for me.[7]

From the age of fourteen onwards he was isolated, cut off entirely from boys of his own age, intellectually dominated by a scholar thirty-five years older than himself, immersed in the solitary task of reading a daunting list of Catholic authorities: Eckstein, Newman, Montalambert, Ventura, Faber, Cullen, Wiseman, Passaglia, Gratry, Dupanloup, De Lucca, De Rossi, Orestes Brownson, Russell, De Buck, Maret, Darboy, Mermillod, Ketteler, Theiner, Veuillot, Windischmann. He met many of these writers, questioned them and, in his own phrase, 'tested' them in the hope that they might throw light on his obsessive concern with the 'wavy line'. It was Döllinger, here as in all else, who kindled this passion for what Acton called the remunerative but perilous field of Church history. Döllinger became the father he never had; it was Döllinger who initiated him into the mysteries of the historical craft, channelled his aggressive all-absorbing intellectual curiosity and, at a stroke, turned night into day. It was Döllinger who in his *History of Christianity* spoke of God as Truth, of providence as 'the fruits of the death of Christ ripening for the world' and of the Catholic Church as sole repository and protector of that divine truth.[8] He had initially fostered a combative ultramontanism at the University of Munich, believing that Bavaria was destined to become the centre of a new Catholic renaissance which would destroy the twin foes of Protestantism and secularism. He urged Catholic scholarship to adopt a militant posture. St Augustine had spoken of the secular state having been born out of fratricide. Now more than ever to retreat into contemplative quietism within the city of God was to concede victory to the temporal powers of the earth. Instead of being defensive and uncertain the Catholic must do battle against unbelief and penetrate the profane world with a renewed Christian spirit. The Church was uniquely qualified for this offensive. Attached to no particular political system, acknowledging no single earthly authority, the Catholic spirit could ally itself with any political force which might advance its cause. Intellectually Catholicism remained unaffected by the assaults of Darwin and of German biblical criticism, for unlike its Protestant foe it did not draw its continuing revelation solely from the Bible. The unique elasticity of its developing faith rendered it immune to clerical scandal or the discovery of rocks and fossils which might challenge the literal interpretation of the book of Genesis.

Acton imbibed this euphoria and in his youthful intoxication believed everything was possible. Together he and Döllinger would launch a crusade of proselytization and conversion and fight the wolves outside the Church. Döllinger was convinced that Protestantism could not long survive the German revolution of 1848; the reunification of the Christian world was imminent, its consummation would be achieved in a matter of decades. He had especially high hopes for England. The influx of Irish immigrants, the spiritual regeneration effected by the Tractarians, the entry of many Anglicans within the Catholic fold and the re-establishment of the Catholic hierarchy in 1850, presaged a Catholic revival similar to that of Bavaria.

Acton returned to England in 1857 buoyed up by these high expectations and absolutely convinced that the interests of his Church coincided with the interests of justice. A precocious young man in his early twenties, his personality was a complex mixture of unquestioning devotion and a quick, impulsive, critical nature. His learning was prodigious, far beyond that of his years, and his reading omnivorous. Granville complained of his stepson's rapidly expanding library, of books piling up in spare rooms and taking over bedrooms. His manner was grave and earnest; he grew a beard. He nurtured deep ambitions; he wished to cut a figure for himself in public life. The young schoolboy who had signed his name 'Caesar Agamemnon' in his letters home had come of age and an intense sense of intellectual superiority had taken grip. That intelligence was ferocious, combative and iconoclastic. In principle it advocated tolerance, but in temperament it was intolerant and doctrinaire and, loath to countenance false gods, it thirsted for enemies to outflank and slaughter.

Repeatedly Döllinger warned him against this, but he continued, in Manning's words, to exhibit 'the inflation of German professors, and the ruthless talk of undergraduates'.[9]

He issued a personal manifesto: 'My principle is: peace among Catholics, for Protestants of goodwill a golden bridge, polemics to be directed chiefly against freethinkers.' In his early journalism Carlyle was condemned as an infidel, who had swallowed German scholarship without its concomitant Catholicism; Ruskin was a prophet with nothing to foretell; Buckle's godless materialism, his emphasis on arid statistical averages in place of the individual's divine free will, was impious and dehumanizing: 'In his laborious endeavour to degrade the history of mankind, and of the dealings of God with man, to the level of one of the natural sciences, he has stripped it of its philosophical, of its divine, and even of its human character and interest.' Comte's misguided attempts to displace God from the centre of the universe and put man in his place were heretical. His demotion of religion to the lowest stage of human advancement – the pandering to a pitiful human need for fiction and superstition – and his drawing up of a Positivist Calendar of great men to replace saints' days, were a deliberate exercise in profanity. Feuerbach's *Essence of Christianity*, while advancing an ingenious theory of the relationship between soul and God, managed to deny the existence of either. John Stuart Mill's utilitarianism, with its modification of a felicific calculus, its attempt to impose a yardstick of human self-indulgence called 'happiness', placed him squarely among secular philosophers whose kingdom was of this world and who ultimately took their moral standards from Machiavelli. For government was not the guarantor of maximum personal happiness, nor the rule of force, nor the consequence of a whig social contract. If, as Mill believed, individual happiness was the true end of society, liberty as such would be unnecessary, for liberty did not make men happy. Liberty was less a demand for rights than a call to duty and the fulfilment of obligations, 'the consequence of the recognition that man must obey the will of God'. Demolishing the secular enemy one by one Acton called for more able and exacting adversaries to rouse his Church from its mental torpor and vindicate its truths. 'The intellectual armour with which the doctrine of the Church is assailed becomes the trophy of her victory. All her battles are defensive, but they all terminate in conquest.'[10]

Contemporary nationalism was the greatest enemy of all because it struck at the very heart of the Catholic Church. Acton's religious beliefs were inseparable from his political thinking, and his understanding and interpretation of current events were shaped principally by his Catholic perception of things. It was because the nation-state threatened to fragment still further the claims of Catholic universalism and advance by political means the spiritual schism of the Reformation that he so vigorously opposed it. Advocates of the state as the highest good not only challenged God but also that individual and earthly dualism – the invisible conscience and the visible Church – ordained by God. At best its implicit Erastianism would chain each national Church to the state: at worst it would destroy the spiritual arm entirely and replace the worship of God with the worship of the state. But the Church was only the greatest of a multitude of moderating, intermediate bodies which would be swept away when the Republic One and Indivisible had succeeded in embodying the supremacy of a collective will which denied that right was superior to authority. In its denial of diversity and harmony, its intolerance of minorities and its crushing conformity, it threatened every precondition of liberty. The Catholic Church's diversity in unity was reflected in the temporal sphere by the multinational states of Austria-Hungary, Great Britain and Switzerland where 'The presence of different nations under the same sovereignty is similar in its effect to the independence of the Church in the State ... and the State which is reluctant to tolerate differences ... must from the same cause interfere in the internal government of religion.'[11]

Nationalism embodied a primitive patriotism which deified material self-interest and self-aggrandizement and knew nothing of higher obligations and duties. It was not surprising that Mill, having argued for the unrestrained pursuit of personal liberty, should, in his *Representative Government* of 1861, go on to defend the collective will of the nation-state as the highest good. Yet this new manifestation of secularism was worshipped as a religion because it truckled to a deep but destructive yearning for perfectionism. Acton attacked the abstract absolutism of Mazzini, the theoretician of Italian unification, who sought through an overwhelming concentration of powers to impose a terrifying uniformity on the Italian state. But his pernicious idealism, his promise of absolute freedom, could lead only to absolute bondage. Catholicism, in contrast, was rooted in the knowledge of original sin; it laboured realistically to assimilate realities with ideas, adjusted gradually to time and circumstance, and made no attempt to achieve an impossible ideal. Church dogmas had grown uninterruptedly: God had decreed a universal order of hierarchy. These principles, converted into practical political concerns, made Acton profoundly conservative and anti-revolutionary when he turned to consider the very direct threat of Italian nationalism to papal power and Catholic Austria.

Even as late as 1861 he continued to defend the Pope's temporal powers as a palpable symbol of the Church's sovereignty on earth. He conceded in a confused manner that this patrimony was accidental rather than essential, a necessity rather than an advantage, inevitable rather than desirable, but he was loath to desert St Peter's sinking ship, and discussed the possibility of spiriting Pius IX away to Bavaria or Spain where he could regroup his forces for a renewed assault on Italian secularism. This doomed, rearguard action in the pages of the Catholic *Rambler* actually placed him closer to the ultramontane Manning, who believed that the extinction of temporal authority would inaugurate the reign of Antichrist, than to Newman, who was indifferent beyond thinking it absurd that the Vicar of Christ should have to depend upon the protection of French bayonets.

A trip to the United States in 1853 in the company of his cousin Lord Ellesmere merely reinforced his conservative bias, serving, as he wrote at the time, as a homeopathic cure against democracy. His *American Diary* reflected at every turn a condescending dismissiveness which disparaged every aspect of republican egalitarianism he came across, and, with the outbreak of civil war eight years later, he interpreted the conflict by extrapolating directly from his European experience and his personal preoccupations. The Southern confederates became a repressed minority; their secession an assertion of independence against the imposition of Northern despotism. The abolitionist displayed all the presumptuous idealism of Mazzini, appealing anarchically beyond the written constitution to a higher law. Like Cavour, the Northern unionists placed equality above liberty and sought to destroy the Southern states' rights because, like the Catholic Church in Europe, they constituted the sole remaining obstacle to absolutism.

In taking up the confederate cause Acton was also obliged to support the right, as John Stuart Mill put it, of slave-owners to burn blacks alive, and in his apology for the 'peculiar institution' he went far further than any other pro-Southern conservative dared. Quoting St Paul, he argued that to suffer and submit was sanctifying, that just as a Christian subject must obey his arbitrary sovereign so the slave must unquestioningly obey his master. He spoke of the blessings of servitude, of bondage as a providential instrument which elicited sacrifice from the slave and charity from the master. And because the Southern minority had in 1861 reasserted the sacred order of inequality, he concluded that slavery was essential to genuine democracy.[12]

This extraordinary line of reasoning illustrates Acton's tendency to begin from liberal premises in order to reach highly illiberal conclusions. Condemning nationalism for crushing racial minorities he ends by justifying the most extreme form of racial domination then in existence. His essay on 'Nationality' of 1862 has been interpreted as a prescient plea for mutual toleration, but its thesis is in essence reactionary, anti-revolutionary and Catholic. He argues negatively against nationalism because of its direct threat to his Church, and positively for pluralism because it would enable his Church to survive. His sustained critique of abstractionalism is itself formulated in highly abstract terms. His plea for diversity ('The combination of different nations in one State is as necessary a condition of civilized life as the combination of men in society') terminates in admiration for the polyglot Austro-Hungarian Empire. Yet this is all the more curious because his detailed 'Notes on the Present State of Austria', gathered from personal contacts and published a year earlier, reveals a real not an idealized empire, fraught with chaos, maladministration and imminent disintegration. He deplores nationalism as the crudest manifestation of racialism – 'no philosophy,' he once wrote, 'is cheaper or more vulgar than that which traces all history to diversities of ethnological type and blend' – yet his own historical assumptions are entirely racial. France, ruled by the mountebank Napoleon, seedbed of freethinkers, anti-clerics and Gallicanism, displays in its history a helpless lurching between libertarianism and despotism, consistent only in its servility and 'unparalleled political incapacity'. Imbibing the whig principles of Englishmen, so much admired by eighteenth-century French thinkers, the Gallic temperament had become intoxicated, subverting the ordered liberties of 1688 and transforming them into the destructive, rootless principles of the Rights of Man and the reign of terror. If France symbolized the revolutionary spirit, England's uniquely uninterrupted growth revealed most clearly the hand of God. Her organic tradition and Catholic spirit were especially evident in the writings of Edmund Burke which, to the youthful Acton, were 'the law and the prophets' and a political bible by which he could repulse the advance of a new, subversive order.[13]

But it was as a historian that Acton felt best qualified to serve his Church, and it is in his historical writings that his Catholic apologetic is most clearly revealed and where his promise of a 'golden bridge' to Protestants is most clearly ignored.

Döllinger had convinced him that for too long Protestant historians like Ranke and Droysen had bent the past to their own cause. Ranke had called history a 'holy hieroglyph' and had set about almost singlehandedly interpreting the divine pattern in time. Yet Acton believed Protestant scholarship was severely handicapped; born in schism, Protestant history became a relentless distortion seeking to justify its initial spiritual breach by emphasizing the absolute corruption and spiritual bankruptcy of the Catholic Church. Catholic historians in turn had failed to realize that history was almost exclusively their own domain; that the European past was predominantly a Catholic past and its heritage was universal and continuous. Newman in his *Development of Doctrine* had charted the authoritative growth of dogma from the direct revelation of the early Fathers down to its majestic deposit in the present day. His book had made fellow Catholics aware of the divine Catholic mission being made explicit through time and of history as the true demonstration of religion. To the believing Acton the issue was absurdly simple: 'No Catholic is as good as his religion. It is the only case in which there is not the slightest inducement to represent friends and enemies otherwise than as they are. Hence perfect impartiality is possible only among Catholics.'[14]

Sixteenth-century Protestants, on the other hand, tended to be identified as precursors of nineteenth-century nationalists, introducing a new abstract intolerance into theological discourse, insisting upon a disruptive atomic freedom which threatened a providential hierarchy. Luther had at first exploited the principle of conscience as a means of legitimizing dissent, but as the solvent schismatic spirit spread among his own ranks, he turned to the aid of princes to sustain his cause. Thereafter Luther preached total submission to orthodox princes and rebellion against heterodox rulers however just, thus combining the extremes of despotism and revolution. The merging of spiritual and secular powers by Melanchthon and Calvin perfected a movement which began by demanding freedom of conscience and ended by denying it. Fusing together a divinely ordained dualism in an absolutist theocratic state they sought to exterminate in the name of God. It was in the rationale rather than in the methods of persecution that Acton attempted to draw the sharpest contrast between the two rival Churches. He insisted that Catholicism persecuted from necessity, for specific, pragmatic political and social reasons, while Protestantism presented a quite novel and distinct spirit of intolerance which was rooted in dogmatic first principles and religious duty. The Catholic Church had begun in unity and freedom; it was the threat that heresy posed to the fabric of Christian society, the threat to authority of part of her community being in spiritual opposition, which compelled her to retaliate. It was for this, and not religious heresy, that the Albigensians were so mercilessly extirpated. He conceded the Church's sanguinary role in Languedoc, Lombardy and Spain but dismissed 'the accidental details attending their practical realization' by insisting that the abstract consistency which led to persecution in Sweden and Germany was of a quite different and unforgivable order. In his review of Hefele's *Life of Cardinal Ximenes* the Spanish prelate was condemned primarily for allowing the Crown to use the machinery of the Inquisition to extend its powers at the expense of the Church. Protestant historians, by concentrating on the 'picturesque details' of those 20,000 'criminals' put to death, had neglected this far more important long-term consequence. In the short term the spiritual police had succeeded in protecting morality, eradicating a wide variety of vices and crimes and transforming the Inquisition into 'the instrument by which greater humanity, morality, and subordination were restored'.[15]

Underlying this analysis was Acton's assumption that persecution was a lesser evil than complete religious liberty. Compulsion and coercion were distasteful, but preferable if a natural, unforced spiritual unity was unobtainable, and here his yearning for spiritual unity went quite contrary to his political pluralism. 'Tolerance of error is requisite for freedom,' he wrote, 'but freedom will be most complete where there is no actual diversity to be resisted, and no theoretical unity to be maintained, but where unity exists as the triumph of truth, not of force, through the victory of the Church, not through the enactment of the State.' Tolerance was equated with indifference, intolerance with sincerity. In an indifferent state ecclesiastical authority could no longer exist for 'religious liberty is not the negative right of being without any particular religion, just as self-government is not anarchy. . . . Far from implying a general toleration, [religious liberty] is best secured by a limited one.'[16]

Just as Acton distanced himself from the bloody regime of Torquemada, systematic torture and the auto-da-fé, so he managed to justify the Church's record by resorting to historical relativism and historical necessity. 'At one period toleration would destroy society; at another, persecution is fatal to liberty.'[17] At this time he held the belief along with Döllinger that history and the historian knew nothing of right or wrong, that moral standards were superfluous. Released from the ethics which burdened his maturity he could spin ingenious arguments in palliation of his Church. His 'Protestant Theory of Persecution' and 'Mr Goldwin Smith's Irish History', both published in the *Rambler* in 1862, were essentially exercises in a latter-day Counter-Reformation. Goldwin Smith's greatest crime seems to have been his dispassion, his merciful judgements, his failure to distinguish between the two Churches and his emphasis on the human and the humane at the expense of the spiritual. But all of Acton's subtle distinctions between political and theological persecution were unreal, for it was clear that the spiritual threat of heresy was indistinguishable from the social and political threat of revolutionary sects under the seamless garment of the Respublica Christiana, that Catholic Europe was no less theocratic than Protestant Europe. The great American medieval scholar Henry C. Lea would later demolish Acton's contention that the Spanish Inquisition was aimed solely at apostates (what of the persecuted Jews and Moors?) and the maintenance of social order. Yet another notable medievalist, G. G. Coulton, continued to believe as late as 1931 that Acton was a staunch liberal ally in his campaign against the current Catholic sophistries of Cardinal Gasquet, Chesterton and Belloc, and in a note in the *English Historical Review* managed to convince himself that the illiberal 'Protestant Theory of Persecution' could not possibly have been written by Acton.

In 1857 Acton travelled with Döllinger to Rome in part to meet Theiner, the Vatican archivist, in the hope of gaining access to the rich store of manuscripts deposited there. Let loose among the records he began to realize that the assertion by the Jesuit historian Perrone that no heretic suffered persecution under the Roman Inquisition was a lie and that the victimization of Giordano Bruno and Galileo was neither accidental nor exceptional. He began to have doubts about his own assertions, taken uncritically from Döllinger, De Maistre and Hefele, that the Spanish Inquisition was motivated solely by *raison d'état* and was carried out entirely by the secular arm. He began to understand that the Inquisitor's plea for mercy on behalf of the condemned heretic was a formal hypocrisy uttered before delivering the victim over to the stake. He came to realize that the Inquisition aimed, primarily, not at combating sin or error, but at enforcing unity, an outward, fictitious unity, in order to promote authority before faith. If St Paul's assertion that the Church 'beareth not the sword in vain; for he is the minister of God, a revenger to execute wrath upon him that doeth evil' (Romans xiii: 4) had been interpreted quite literally since the days of Theodosius, it followed that mercy to heretics was disobedience to God and that the most revered figures of the Church – Saints Dominic and Francis, Bernard, Bonaventura, Thomas Aquinas – were all implicated in the act of persecution. If the Church had, of free choice, collaborated in the setting up of this hideous apparatus in order to apply its tremendous powers over pain, death and hell, then it followed that 'what happened is not assignable to invincible causes, and history must turn from general and easy explanation to trace the sinuosities of a tangled thread'.[18]

Wherever he turned in the archives this same question of personal responsibility crowded in upon him along with the even greater question of historical responsibility. Each new piece of fresh documentary evidence questioned the veracity and motives of Church historians, and this was all the more catastrophic to Acton because he had so desperately wished to affirm orthodoxy. Years later he spoke of his 'infinite credulity and trust', of his having to overcome 'a strong tendency to hero worship and reverence', of having always respected men until he found them out. 'But when I came to study and judge for myself I found that what they told me and preached and wrote was, on many decisive questions, false ... I came, very slowly and reluctantly indeed, to the conclusion that they were dishonest.'[19] He had planned a vindication of Pallavicino's orthodox account of the Council of Trent written in 1656–57 as a refutation of Paolo Sarpi's record of 1619 which was 'the great arsenal for all the enemies of the Church'. He ended by questioning both. Here the seeds of self-doubt were sown and the journey from engagement to disengagement, from interested Catholic to disinterested historian, began. This revelation inaugurated, in Acton's own phrase, 'the epoch of emancipation'. If Sarpi's critical account had a measure of truth in it and if Pallavicino's interpretation was intended to buttress the Church and justify the Tridentine decrees, then historical truth was a more complex matter and did not reside exclusively within the body of one Church. Worse still, what if the Church had deliberately falsified history, had systematically distorted and perverted, forged documents, erased others, to subordinate it to the supreme demands of dogma and statecraft? The pursuit of historical truth was to transform Acton from a vehement apologist to an equally vehement advocate of impartiality, and lead him to attack the greater enemy within rather than the lesser enemy without.

3   The Liberal Catholic

It was, he insisted, 'a very simple, obvious and not interesting story. It is the story of a man who started in life believing himself a sincere Catholic and a sincere Liberal; who therefore renounced everything in Catholicism which was not compatible with Liberty, and everything in Politics which was not compatible with Catholicity ... That is my entire Capital.'[1] This is how Acton sketched out his life to Charlotte Blennerhassett in 1879. But it was not quite so straightforward as that, for truth is rarely simple, nor was his stance obvious, because it left him quite isolated from his co-religionists; and the story, involving as it does a painful growth towards a degree of self-understanding, is not uninteresting.

The 1860s were a momentous stage in Acton's intellectual and emotional development. They were years characterized by intense activity, when he threw himself into journalism and archival research and dabbled in politics with seemingly limitless energy. The decade began in high hopes and generous gestures. His engagement to the Countess Marie von Arco-Valley in 1864 brought a new joy into his life. From Döllinger he had learned the hard lessons of long study and endurance; Marie had now to teach him the art of bearing prosperity. From Naples in January 1865 he writes daily to his betrothed, opening each letter with conventional epistolary sighs: 'How is it possible the girl I have loved so well should be so good to me! Make me worthy of it, Dearest, and let me hope, through you, to be brought nearer to you, and made more able to preserve your happiness when it will be all my care.'[2] He is staying with his grandmother, widow of the Commander who had drunk deep into the night in Gibbon's company. He makes arrangements to have his uncle, the Cardinal, brought back to be buried in the family chapel at Aldenham. Meanwhile it is carnival time in Naples. He visits Herculaneum and unrolls illegible manuscripts burned almost to a cinder. An expedition is made on donkeys to the Camaldoli convent in the hills overlooking the beautiful, expansive bay. By May he is back in St James's Place in London. He has dined with the Count of Paris, made the acquaintance of the beautiful Lady Dufferin, attended a grand ball graced by the Prince and Princess of Wales and had a long and interesting conversation with Disraeli before ordering his carriage at 2 am.

Despite the many disappointments and the rebuffs and challenges from authority his high spirits were sustained throughout these difficult years, because Döllinger had encased his pupil's faith in an impregnable intellectual armour. His sense of the absolute rightness of his cause endowed him with a supreme self-confidence which remained unshaken during a time of increasing religious doubt and loss of faith. Many of his contemporaries were suspended agonizingly between the need to believe and the increasing difficulty of belief, aware of a spiritual void left by the passing of 'lost sanctions and banished hopes'. It was the decade of Darwin's *Origin of Species* (1859), of a new biblical criticism which challenged Anglican orthodoxy and infused the controversial *Essays and Reviews* (1860), of Bishop Colenso of Natal's nagging doubts about the authenticity of the Pentateuch and his growing suspicion that the Zulus he had been sent to convert might be right and he wrong. In the midst of all this relentless questioning and upheaval, Acton remained unaffected, secure in the knowledge that God was truth and that 'the full exposition of truth is the great object for which the existence of mankind is prolonged on earth'. Because the Catholic Church was the unique repository of divine truth it followed that it could best flourish in an atmosphere of free discussion and intellectual enquiry. True scholars of the Church, unlike scholastics or apologists, were not fearful of advancing science but rather encouraged it, convinced that further advances and fresh discoveries were not incompatible with the divine ordinance but could only add to the greater glory of God and serve ultimately as a safeguard against unbelief. In his review of Döllinger's *History of Christianity* in 1861 he spoke of liberty as the medium of faith, 'and inasmuch as ignorance and error cannot permanently be kept asunder, inasmuch as truth belongs to the nature of God, and religion is allied with all truths and contradicted by all errors, the Church is not only the enemy of falsehood, but indirectly, though necessarily, the promoter of all knowledge. She not only does not fear its increase, but requires it.'[3]

But the Church was not only truth, it was also morality, deriving its eternal system of ethics from Christ's Beatitudes and the Sermon on the Mount. More especially Acton took for his text St Paul's admonition to the Romans that 'All that is not the outcome of faith is sin.' That is, and the gloss is his own, 'Faith must be sincere. When defended by sin it is not sincere; theologically, it is not Faith. God's grace does not operate by sin.' He believed that within an infallible Church an individual was more likely to be led astray by sin than by error; here untruthfulness, not untruth, was the greater enemy, not erring conscience, but the lack of one. To commit sin was to know right and yet, knowingly, act wrongly. Vice was, then, an active and voluntary repudiation of grace and of conscience, and the greatest vices of all were spiritual. Temporal powers were ultimately limited and transient, placed in time and of this world. Their misuse by autocrats like Nero, Ivan the Terrible and Louis XIV, or by democrats such as Mazzini or St Just, were as nothing beside spiritual despotism. For such powers were timeless, reaching beyond earth into the hereafter, binding or loosing for eternity, choosing to open or close the gates of heaven and hell. Such omnipotent resources were terrifying to contemplate and when abused of the essence of evil. Too often spiritual authority had confused ends and means, been prompted by mixed motives to employ dubious methods to achieve a desired good, and while religion was, as he stated at the beginning of his lecture on 'The History of Freedom', the motive of all good deeds, it was also the common pretext for crimes committed in the name of God, more especially the doing of great wrongs for the sake of saving souls. Acton recoiled in horror from such spiritual perversion which deprived its victims of grace, corroded the soul of the persecutor and corrupted the faith of the Church. This warped morality touched the conscience; it was 'an agency constantly active, pervading life, penetrating the soul by many channels, in almost every sermon and in almost every prayer book': it was sacrilegious.[4]

Because he became convinced that the ultramontanes threatened truth and morality in the Church he became their implacable enemy. He dated the origins of that movement and its deviation from the scriptural codes in the seventh to eleventh centuries, culminating in the pontificate of the powerful and aggressive Hildebrand, Gregory VII (1073–85), who had fought through the investiture controversy for the omnipotence of the spiritual arm, the universal extension of the Christian empire and the concentration of powers in the hands of the Pontiff. Attacked by the Reformation, the ultramontane spirit once more revived and in its sixteenth-century counteroffensive against Protestantism equipped itself with an 'austere immorality'. The Council of Trent cemented an unholy alliance with the secular powers. Calling upon princes to exterminate the enemy the Church became 'the gilded crutch of absolutism' at a time when 'Calvin preached and Bellarmine lectured, but Machiavelli reigned'.[5] Because the Scriptures were the strongest weapon the Lutherans could wield against authority, the Church retreated from them – 'subjugated' them, in Acton's phrase – and retreated to the impregnable ground of dogma. Then once again in his own day, following the maelstrom of the French Revolution and the Napoleonic conquests, ultramontanism gained an unprecedented hold. In its modern phase its philosopher and refounder was Joseph De Maistre (1753–1821). He had been appalled by the spiritual chaos and social upheaval of the period and as one of its victims had been forced to flee into exile as the advancing French republicans had invaded and annexed his native Savoy.

He came to blame this universal anarchy on individual sin and the weakness of the ruling powers. Henceforth he wished to reknit the threads of the past, reject revolution, constitutionalism, even counter-revolution, and cast instead the shadow of the executioner over society to compel absolute obedience and order. In his volume on *The Pope* of 1819 he argued for an unquestioning infallibility in the spiritual realm to parallel absolutism in the state. He wished above all to dethrone reason, for the desiccating reasoning of the Enlightenment had led to revolution, and replace it with an unreasoning and conforming faith. After De Maistre neo-Catholicism became locked into a conspiracy against truth; belief, not objective fact, was its prime objective, and everything which did not minister to the salvation of man and the promotion of the Church was superfluous. Its direct appeal to the dictates of the believing heart extended beyond dogma into the domain of politics. It insisted, for example, that the Pontiff's temporal powers could no more be questioned than could the doctrine of the Holy Trinity. Regressive scholasticism was accompanied by political reaction and the wish to revive an impossible lost Catholic unity. 'In the presence of anarchy they sought a remedy in despotism: they opposed modern unbelief with an exploded superstition, and strove to expel the new devil with the old one.'[6]

Acton rapidly became convinced that the ultramontane conspiracy was concentrated on historical science. Of course, like any other large institution, the Church was sensitive to criticism, shrank from scrutiny and denied responsibility for past errors and wrongs. But this abhorrence was more than just sensitivity; it was the irrefutable obstinacy of historical facts, their independence and autonomy, their very uncontrollability, which fed the suspicion of ultras. To reveal that the Church had changed through history, that it had held opinions in the past which had been disregarded, was to question the Church's authentic voice in the present. 'The Church,' he realized,

felt no desire to know its own past – to meditate its experience. Negation of history took its place. It was argued
that there was no need to look behind the present scenes.
Things were right because they were. The life of the Church
is our guide, the tacit sanction of custom. To look further
is to call up the dead authorities against the living in order
to arbitrate between them ... So that the appeal to history,
unless as a controversy with Protestants, concealed a
flavour of opposition and doubt; promoted uncertainty.[7]

In the hands of the ultramontane history became a tool to
distort, suppress, subordinate, and no longer an independent,
disinterested pursuit. Exploiting historical ignorance Jesuit
scholars subtly shifted ground from the denial of certainty
to the denial of truth, and engaged in falsehoods and calumny.
Guéranger, for example, revived the myth of Pope Sylvester's
baptism of Constantine; Wilhelm von Schütz cleared the
Catholic faction of complicity in the St Bartholomew
Massacre, and Father Perrone, one of the masters of 'the
unscrupulous school', resurrected the lie that Calvin died of
syphilis. Acton's struggle with authority, then, was on two
levels; he opposed as a Catholic the Pope's self-aggrandizement and as a historian that section of the Church which
refused to be bound by the evidence of the past: 'the antagon-
ism is against historical science chiefly ... The Roman
authority is attacked by Scripture and Tradition. That is, by
the historical sciences, and political. Against these his bitter-
ness is directed.'[8]

'He' was Giovanni Maria Mastai-Ferretti (1792–1878),
elevated to the papal chair as Pius IX in 1846. Like Acton he
had undergone his own homeopathic cure against democracy
in 1848 when he was forced to flee into temporary exile at
Gaeta in the wake of nationalist revolution. But on his return
to Rome in 1850, and unlike Acton, he was never again to
dally with the dangerous forces of liberalism, but proceeded
instead to surround himself with Jesuits (the order had been
refounded in 1814) and high ultras such as Antonelli, Talbot

and Barnabo, and prepare his ground carefully for the final triumph of papal authority. 'Pio Nono', as he was called in Italian, combined a degree of cunning statecraft with a faith rooted in superstition. As a young man he had been cured of epilepsy praying at the Blessed Virgin Mary's shrine at Loreto. He was vouchsafed nightly visitation by St Philomena who confirmed the wisdom of his policies. Lord Odo Russell, the unofficial British representative to the Vatican, dismissed him as that 'great Mumbo Jumbo', and Acton too, in his audience of 1857, seems not to have taken the full measure of his enemy: 'My impression is not of any ability and he seems less banally good-natured than his smiling pictures represent him to be.'[9] For as his earthly powers ebbed away so Pius consistently extended his spiritual control. He moved swiftly to censure the liberal Catholic congresses at Malines in August 1863 and in Munich in September of the same year. Sustained by an extraordinary welling up of mysticism and religious hysteria he unilaterally proclaimed the dogma of the Immaculate Conception in his *Ineffabilis Deus* of 1854, a decision divinely confirmed by the Blessed Virgin Mary herself when she appeared and spoke before Bernadette Soubirous at Lourdes four years later. In 1864 he consolidated his position in the bull *Quanta Cura* which appended a *Syllabus Errorum* which included pantheism, naturalism, rationalism, indifferentism, latitudinarianism, socialism and communism. The last and greatest error of all was that the Pope 'can and ought to reconcile himself to, and come to terms with, progress, liberalism and modern civilization'. A year later he appointed Henry Edward Manning, the leading English ultra, to succeed Wiseman as Archbishop of Westminster. The battle lines were drawn up.

Acton fought this new, aggressive Vaticanism directly through his liberal Catholic journalism at home and indirectly through his archival researches abroad. Nowhere more than in England was it necessary to rouse what he took to be an illiterate episcopate, an ignorant clergy and a prejudiced and lethargic laity, seemingly unaware of the imperative mission

of reconciling religion and truth, theology and history. Some
converts had lapsed into the theatrical Romanism of Father
Faber and the London Oratory with its Brotherhood of the
Will of God, its cult of the Blessed Blood and of the Virgin
Mary (it was rumoured that Faber sometimes referred to her
casually as 'dearest mama'). Having appointed John Brande
Morris as his estate chaplain at Aldenham, Acton suffered
from the excesses of this school at first hand and it was not
until his bishop, Brown of Shrewsbury, wrote a letter of censure on Morris's style of preaching, which 'not only awakened
the curiosity of young people, and tore away the veil from
their imagination, but habituated all the congregation to hear
the most sacred things, and Our Lady in particular, associated
with ideas hardly ever expressed out of a medical school',
that Morris could be prevailed upon to depart.[10] Manning
proved a far more formidable adversary because he controlled
the orthodox Catholic press, the *Tablet* and the *Dublin
Review*, and through Monsignor Talbot at Rome had direct
access to power. Acton's initial impression had been favourable, but it rapidly gave way to mutual suspicion and hatred
as he discovered Mephistophelian depths in the Archbishop,
who in turn espied a conspirator in the dark whom he came
to loathe more than any Protestant or atheist living.

Between both stood the complex and subtle Newman. In
many ways he should have sided automatically with Acton.
He was benign and tolerant by temperament, they collaborated together on the new university in Dublin and launched
liberal Catholic journalism in England. Newman opposed
papal aggrandizement and was deeply injured by the deliberate frustrating of his priestly career by Manning, who dismissed him contemptuously as representing 'the old Anglican,
patristic, literary, Oxford tone translated into the church'.[11]
But these similarities were in part, at least, superficial and
disguised more fundamental differences. For if Newman was
liberal by temperament his liberality rested on a theoretical
authoritarianism. Acton, in contrast, was dogmatic in character and a doctrinaire liberal, and this was the source of

all the difficulties surrounding their long relationship. Fundamental too was the fact that Newman knew no German and little of German scholarship and, unlike Acton, could not indulge in the irresponsibilities of laymanship.

At a stroke Newman's conversion of 1845 had resolved the multitude of difficulties and doubts that had hitherto assailed him. A final chapter in his *Apologia* made abundantly clear that he had entered Rome 'to withstand and baffle the fierce energy of passion and the all-corroding, all-dissolving scepticism of the intellect in religious inquiries'. What he was escaping from were precisely those characteristics of liberalism, its rationalism, its anti-dogmatism, its pluralistic tolerance, what Newman called the 'suicidal excesses' of its persistent questioning, which Acton held most dear. Newman believed truth to be the object of reason, but for fallen man reason led too readily to unbelief, and in exchanging doubt for certainty, fallible humanism for infallible authority, he was confirming the self-same motivation which led to Manning's conversion ('Rome or licence of thought and will') six years later. Thereafter while he might believe authority misguided and heavy-handed in its use of power he never once denied its right to exercise it, nor ceased to believe that the Catholic had no choice but to submit and obey. Christ was prophet and priest, but he was also king who through the body of his visible Church exerted a universal, imperial sway. While he continued to take a lively and acute interest in passing events his retreat into the Birmingham Oratory reflected a habit of mind which was essentially theological and contemplative. He became wholly absorbed in the relationship between God and his own soul. Between them, and on earth, lay an abyss, the consequence of a terrible primal calamity, a fall from grace in which Newman saw the world devoid of its creator. Given such soul-disturbing insights he frequently chided Acton for his uncertain intrusions into theology, while the historian's fascination with intrigue, violence and the 'wavy line' of ecclesiastical policy struck him as curiously naive and beside the point. That God's truth was carried in earthen vessels seemed obvious and unsurprising: 'to touch politics was to touch pitch,' and that was that.[12]

Acton was in turn disturbed by what he took to be Newman's quietism and indifference to mundane political matters. It was shocking, when he was fighting so hard for the temporal power in the pages of the *Rambler*, to receive news of the MP who travelled to Edgbaston to solicit Newman's stand on the matter: 'What times we live in Father Newman! Look at all that is going on in Italy.' 'Yes indeed!' came the reply. 'And look at China too, and New Zealand!' Again, despite his opposition to the proposed promulgation of papal infallibility in 1869, Newman was content to plead age and the malaria of a Roman summer as an excuse for absenting himself, content only to add that the forthcoming council could err, unless, of course, the Holy Ghost prevented it. When the Vatican decrees confirmed the dogma he merely commented that it was God's will since it was done. In time this disengaged fatalism and infuriating equivocation came to be interpreted by Acton more harshly as casuistry and masterly evasion. Too frequently he eluded definition, escaped the net, maddeningly refused to be placed. A sentence in one of Newman's earliest letters says it all: 'Putting aside the grounds of principle, on which I think we agree, I wished to consider expedience.' This set the tone throughout, with the historian searching always for the firm line, and the priest for the inoffensive, emollient middle ground. And as Acton's isolation soured him and his principles hardened Newman was transformed into 'that splendid sophist', that 'most cautious and artful of apologists' who was 'heart and soul, far more than he ever suffered to appear, an advocate of Rome'. So that by the 1880s when Acton wrote to Creighton insisting that he had 'contrived the gentlest formula of disagreement in coupling you with Cardinal Newman' he was being (though Creighton was unaware of it) savagely sardonic.[13]

The gulf was widest in their separate and distinct understanding of history. At first Acton praised Newman's *Essay on the Development of Christian Doctrine* of 1845. Its opening words – 'Christianity has been long enough in the world to justify us in dealing with it as a fact in the world's history' – thrilled the aspiring historian. He believed that the Jesuit scholars who were disturbed by the book, Perrone and Passaglia, had been displaced by the historian. Then he began to express doubts. 'Development, at first sight, is the reign of History. It could be made to dethrone History. The Reign of the Present.' 'It emancipated him from History and made authority reigned [sic]. It was the voice of the present Church superseding the study of the Past.' Finally, 'Authority, the certain legitimacy and rectitude of its acts, became his centre-piece and refuge. This is what development pointed to.' Because Newman had been prompted to write the *Essay* in order to assimilate the very different teaching of the early Church with its nineteenth-century counterpart by means of dogmatic development, he had ended by asserting not the scientific independence of history but the providential, infallible voice of the Church in 1845. More generally Acton came to appreciate that Newman assigned a very limited role to history; it dealt only with hypotheses and probabilities, unlike belief which was grounded in certitude. It was impossible to dispense personal blame in such complicated matters as the St Bartholomew Massacre when all sides, Protestant and Catholic alike, were motivated by mortal fear of the enemy. Because theology was a matter of revelation it was not subject to factual evidence or proof, and in his *Letter Addressed to His Grace the Duke of Norfolk* (1875) there was a strongly implied criticism of Acton and Döllinger for presuming to stray into personal judgements in Church history which he considered as unlawful as private judgements in the interpretation of Scripture without the guidance of divine authority.[14] Assigning historical responsibility was not only illicit, it was irrelevant. Why, he enquired, should each Catholic be held answerable for the papacy's past wrongdoings? As well hold railway stock-holders responsible for a railway accident, or Queen Victoria for the sins of her uncles. Finally, while Acton discerned the hand of God in history, Newman decidedly did not. Apart from the individual soul, that is apart from biography, history was a world without God, a world which mocked and depressed Newman. 'Note that Newman denies the divine government of the world. Providence does not manifest itself in history. The law of progress is not the law of history.' To Acton, however, 'providence means progress. Notion that God is active in history, that Christ pursues his work among men. That this action is not wasted ... Not to believe in providence is to question the divine government.'[15] For Acton history was not separate from revelation, rather it was the only unassailable revelation vouchsafed to man on earth, and because truth was a question of objective evidence and because no ecclesiastical exigence could alter a fact, the sacredness of historical criticism must be inviolate.

Acton's rocky excursion into the field of journalism served mainly to confirm his suspicion that the ultramontane conspiracy flourished in the present, and out of his personal persecution grew paranoia. Acton became contributor and part-owner of the *Rambler* in 1858 through the influence of Richard Simpson, who had been writing for it since 1848. The two became intimate friends, diverting their boyish enthusiasm for damming up streams in the park at Aldenham into posing as daring *enfants terribles* running amok among the outraged Catholic establishment. The venture was one of crisis following upon crisis, of evaporating funds, of attacks by the orthodox *Dublin Review*, of repeated attempts to meet objections from authority which were never wholly successful, so that there were frequent delations of particular articles to Rome and sharp censure from the pulpit of Westminster. The troubled history is reflected in the constant, erratic turnover of editors and sub-editors – John Moore Capes, James Northcote, Richard Simpson, Thomas Wetherell, Acton, Newman himself, and the equally rapid change of title from *Rambler* (1848–62) to *Home and Foreign* (1862–64) to *Chronicle* (1867–68) and finally to *North British Review* (1869–71), as each journal was launched with fresh funds, high hopes and a new cover only to break up upon the shoals of ecclesiastical disapproval. Newman groaned like an old woman with toothache; he had been severely reprimanded for daring to suggest that the lay community should be consulted in matters of faith during his brief tenure of the editorship in 1859. Now he urged moderation, fearing retaliation because of his exposed position, and worrying that his plan for creating a centre of Catholic learning at his beloved Oxford might miscarry. To no avail. The contributors continued to trace Jansenist heresies to St Augustine, interfered in the dangerous domain of denominational education, would even, Newman wryly observed, drag past papal scandals into footnotes to a treatise on conic sections. Attempts to divert the mischievous Simpson into the safer waters of Shakespearian scholarship failed and Newman's temper snapped. 'I don't wonder at a saying which I hear repeated of a Dominican, that he would like to have the burning of the author.'[16] This chance remark lodged in Acton's memory and was to be recalled thirty years later.

Acton's archival trips of 1857, 1864–65 and 1866–67 reinforced the conclusion drawn from his contemporary journalism: that the spirit which harried the *Rambler* was not a current aberration but part of a far wider pattern of Church censorship of which he was only the most recent and insignificant victim. One by one from 1830 onwards the records of dispossessed dynasties were opened up as each state came to fear that its enemies' account would hold sway. For the first time the researcher could reach beyond secondary materials, 'the careful and easy produce of libraries', to state papers and yet further still to private despatches and letterbooks, to expose the false bottoms of doctored documents, the unpremeditated self-revelation of letters and the unguarded fragments written in the margins of memoranda. In Vienna he found the Toscarini papers; in Venice he explored the archives of the Frari and the Doge's palace. Then on to Rome where he spent three winters rummaging through the Oratorian library and the Jesuit church, the Barberini, Chigi and Caetain papers, and transcribing some of the 8,000 volumes in that 'treasure house of secret history', the Vatican archives. He sought out fresh material on the Council of Trent: from a private diary in Sutton Coldfield, in the Bodleian Library, Oxford, the British Museum library, in Naples, Bergamo, Florence, Munich, Antwerp and Cologne. In pursuit of the Gonzaga papers he met defeat. 'It was early October. Mantua stands in a marsh; there were no muslin curtains, and there was no sleep. After two nights spent with a slipper in my hand, diversifying the wall pattern with mosquito squash, I fled to the comforts of Venice.' He failed to consult the vast collection of Spanish state papers at Simanças and materials at Turin and Genoa which he only later realized held vital clues for the Tridentine Church, but in all he had consulted over forty major collections, some transcripts, such as those copied from originals in the Louvre which had been later destroyed by the Communards, surviving to mellow like an irreplaceable and priceless port. These jaunts also brought him into personal contact with a distant but still-recollected past. In Venice the English historian Rawdon Brown introduced him to Madame Imocenigo who had let her palazzo to Lord Byron and had danced with the last Doge; the librarian at Modena spoke of the last Duc d'Este, Ercole III, who had lost his kingdom at the treaty of Campoformio and died in 1803.

These travels also brought him into vital contact with librarians like Arneth in Vienna and Theiner in Rome who held the keys to the past and who, Acton was convinced, were guardians appointed as much to conceal as to reveal. These minotaurs of the labyrinth fed his fantasies of concealment, his conviction that there were vast conspiracies of silence, and of mysteries determinedly shrouded. He cast himself in the role of a knight, a Childe Roland who sets out in perilous search of the Dark Tower, negotiating all manner of dangers, more especially adversaries disguised as friends, in pursuit of his quest. It required the assistance of the Prussian historian Droysen to gain access to the Berlin state archives where the 'enmity between the truth of history and the reason of state

... lasted longer'. Theiner's function was 'to bar the little door in the winding staircase up which he lived against the just and the unjust'. Sent by the French to spy on the papal court, he was exposed by Cardinal Bernetti and allowed to continue on the understanding that he show his reports before sending them off. Thus Theiner served and betrayed two masters impartially. Acton got his permission to read the despatches of Salviati, the papal nuncio in Paris during the age of Catherine de Medici. But was he shown everything? 'It was impossible to be quite sure of my friend.' Acton had the means of checking. As a result of the Napoleonic conquests the papers had been removed to the Louvre. Chateaubriand copied them out and Sir James Mackintosh used them extensively in his *History of England*. In 1869–70 when the Tridentine precedent suddenly took on great relevance, Theiner was instructed to keep the conciliar documents securely hid. They were leaked from a rare copy in Munich, but thereafter the Vatican archivist was disgraced and the door between his apartments and the Archivo Segreto sealed up. Later that same year when the French garrison abandoned the city and the nationalist forces were closing in, Acton was reputed to have forgone a meeting with Ranke and turned instead to Rome in the hope of entering the unprotected library and securing the *Liber Diurnus* which recorded and anathematized the Monothelite heresies of Pope Honorius I in the seventh century, and which could be used to sabotage the new dogma of papal infallibility. Acton's cousin Minghetti informed the Italian troops and the historian was held in temporary custody outside the city. But that sudden flight to Rome, the walled door, even the mosquito-ridden and sleepless nights, were palpable symbols of a very real crusade of disclosure. The enemy hid the evidence because exposure would be damaging. 'History,' he wrote, 'is much more abominable than we all imagine.' So be it. The task was luminously clear.

There is no other way to compel assent, or to crush interest and prejudice. To renounce the pains and penalties of exhaustive research is to remain a victim to ill informed and designing writers, and to authorities who have worked for ages to build up the vast tradition of conventional mendacity. By going on from book to manuscript and from library to archive, we exchange doubt for certainty, and become our own masters. We explore a new heaven and a new earth, and at each step forward, the world moves with us.[17]

It merely remained for the great book to be written. He planned a life of Cardinal Pole, a history of the Council of Trent and another on the Roman Index: 'everything clusters beautifully around,' he wrote with dazzling confidence to Wetherell in 1864, *'The Censures of Rome and their Influence on Modern Literature*. London. 1866.'[18] This, like all the other projects, remained unwritten, but he did embark upon preliminary historical skirmishes in the pages of the *Rambler*. He began by dropping the euphemistic convention of referring to Paul III's sons as 'nephews'. Goaded by the *Syllabus of Errors* and more especially by the canonization of Peter Arbues (1441–85), the Inquisitor General of Aragon, in 1867, he wrote an article in September of that year on the German Cardinal, Nicholas of Cusa (1400–64). From it the Cardinal emerges as a precursor of papal anti-infallibilism, a minimalist who rejected the Donation of Constantine and the False Decretals as fabrications designed to bestow limitless powers on the Pontiff and who in his *De Concordantia Catholica* of 1433 urged a prescient conciliar alternative in deciding matters of faith. In March of the same year an article on Paolo Sarpi depicted his would-be assassins receiving papal protection, and the Pope, Pius V, and the then Archbishop of Milan, Charles Borromeo, supporting a decree of Lucca which pardoned the murder of citizens who had fled the state as heretics. But in his attempt to indict two saints of the Church Acton overstepped the evidence and made a number of remarkable errors. The decree was in fact passed during the pontificate of Pius IV and not Pius V; he quoted the wrong decree, that of 10 January 1562 instead of 19 December 1561, and anyhow the latter made no provision for the lawful killing of heretics as Acton asserted. More extraordinarily Acton based his evidence not on primary but on secondary sources, in particular Cesare Cantù's *History of Italy*, which he afterwards admitted he had not consulted for over a year and which, when he had reviewed it for the *Chronicle*, he had dismissed as flawed and inaccurate. He afterwards admitted he had got the wrong Pope, but refused to apologize publicly, insisting that the spirit of the Lucca laws was implied in the Roman Inquisition strengthened under Pius v.[19]

Undismayed, he turned to expose further secrets and, his zeal outrunning discretion, if no skeleton could be found in the cupboard, one would have to be placed there. One such was enticingly dangled before him by the shady librarian of the Gesù church in Rome, Joseph Boero. Acton had first met him in Rome in 1857. In 1861 he resurfaced, writing to ask for money from a Catholic barrister from Dorset, Charles Weld, in return for letters purportedly written by Charles II to his alleged illegitimate son, James de la Cloche. These letters had already been dismissed as patent forgeries by John Lingard, another Catholic historian. But egged on by the ever mischievous Simpson, Acton swallowed the letters whole and wrote up a picturesque farrago of nonsense which followed James from his birth in Jersey to Hamburg where he was converted by Queen Christina of Sweden and assured of his princely status, and, after a period as Jesuit novice in Rome, returned to England in disguise to act as his father's confessor (his father having already secretly converted to Rome) and with him played a crucial role in framing the secret Anglo-French treaty of Dover of 1670. Quite apart from exhibiting a complete lack of feel for the period and of the basic historical sense of what is possible and what is not, the historian who had once magisterially stated that 'there is no palliation of inaccuracy' committed a number of elementary howlers on the solid ground of dates alone. Confirmation of James's royal birth, for example, is dated Whitehall, 27 September

1665, at a time when the court had abandoned plague-ridden London for Oxford. Similarly Charles writes of his mother, Henrietta Maria, being present in 1668, when she had left England permanently in 1665. The entire episode displayed an abysmal combination of irresponsible ingenuity, a straining after dramatic effect ('to introduce the Neapolitan story at the moment of [James's] disappearance from the documents would be a stroke of art'), and an ingenuous gullibility which augured ill for the far more serious and major historical essay on the St Bartholomew Massacre of 1869.[20]

The subject was irresistible: it was fraught with duplicity and secrecy, it illustrated perfectly the militancy of the Counter-Reformation Church at its most pitiless, and the whole question of responsibility was obfuscated by a thick layer of contradictory historical interpretation. The legitimist school, for example, had absolved the Crown of responsibility for the massacre and blamed it instead on the ferocious Guise–Coligny vendetta. Catholic historians in turn had implicated the Protestant Henry of Navarre who had encouraged the massacre in a bid to discredit the royal family and eliminate the Catholic Guise faction. But by 1869 historians as varied as Ranke, Falloux, Lingard and Michelet had all added the weight of their authority to an orthodoxy which interpreted the massacre as a sudden, panic decision taken by Catherine de Medici and Charles IX following upon the unsuccessful attempt on Coligny's life on 22 August 1572. Extraordinarily and despite this consensus, Acton returned to the earliest Protestant explanation of a diabolical plot, the Black Legend of a cold, premeditated design to lure the leading Huguenots together in Paris under the pretext of the Valois–Navarre marriage of 18 August and, lulled by the festivities, systematically to exterminate them. Acton made some minor modifications. While the legend had traced the plot back to the Council of Trent or to the meeting between Catherine de Medici and Alva at Bayonne in 1565, he argued that the plot had only taken final form in February 1572 with the defeat of the Huguenot Genlis and Catherine's decision to throw in her lot with the Guise faction at home and the Catholic League abroad. Thereafter she cunningly planned the assassination of Coligny as a preliminary to ringing the tocsin in Paris and extending the liquidation of her Protestant subjects systematically throughout the provinces.

Acton could resurrect this conspiracy theory with some degree of plausibility, for after the event Catherine spoke of a prearranged massacre to gain the approval of Rome and Madrid. But he left many more problems unanswered. He appreciated that Catherine was motivated predominantly by domestic political considerations, that her aim had traditionally been to play off the two factions against each other in the hope of neutralizing them, avoiding civil war and maintaining royal control. If this were so then the wholesale destruction of one faction was an unwise departure: the Crown became instantly threatened, civil war could once more break out, and she would be subjected to the ambitious Guise family at home and to Philip ii of Spain abroad. In fact she tried desperately, following the massacre, to re-establish royal neutrality and a balance between the contending factions, negotiating with the German princes, with William of Orange and with her Protestant subjects at La Rochelle. The Valois–Navarre marriage was itself symbolic of this royal policy. And why, if a general massacre was planned, was Coligny singled out for attack on the 22nd? If the assassination had succeeded the Huguenots, forewarned, would have had time to flee Paris for safety. Acton wrote ominously of the large number of troops billeted in the capital, but Coligny's imminent expedition to the Low Countries was sufficient to explain their presence. He writes of oral orders – no written evidence was extant – by the Crown for the provincial massacres, but the staggered outbreaks throughout the cities of France fit perfectly the time it took to carry the news from province to province. Even Acton remained troubled by the fact that neither Philip ii nor Alva seemed aware of the plot, and presumably if Catherine had promised a great extirpation of Protestants the Pope would in turn have granted a dispensation for the arranged marriage, which, however, was never forth-coming.

But in the article these and other niggling contradictions were not pursued, and throughout Acton displayed a lack of historical nuance and a determined mishandling of sources. With the endemic chaos and bloodletting following the death of Henry II in 1559, rumour was rife in France, and plot answered by counterplot. Talk of plans to assassinate Coligny was legion. But time and time again Acton took rumour for fact and confused plans for the specific assassination with the general massacre. He also wilfully manipulated his mater-ials. Of the two Venetian ambassadors present in Paris, Cavalli and Michiel, he chose to give credence to the latter who argued for premeditation and neglected the former who did not. His star witness, Salviati, the papal nuncio, became 'the strongest witness against the court and the church'. His evidence? Partly Catherine's testimony that Salviati was privy to the plot; but was this daughter of Machiavelli a reliable witness, particularly when it was in her interest, after the event, to convince the Pope of a glorious and premeditated massacre? In fact during the events of 24 and 25 August the nuncio had specifically reported back to the Vatican that there would have been no massacre if the assassination attempt had not failed. The his-torian Henry White had cited this evidence and Acton himself quoted from the very same page on which this statement occurred when he reviewed White's book a year earlier. Yet this anti-premeditation evidence is omitted from the article. Clearly Acton had forced his material into a preconceived framework. Having got so close to the more plausible explana-tion of events to which all the material tended to lead – that Catherine panicked and sounded the tocsin in a desperate bid to liquidate a disastrous expedition to Flanders, avoid civil war and reassert her authority over both son and subjects – he retreats. He retreats because to concede a sudden decision was to confirm the orthodox Catholic version, and this he would not do. 'If no premeditation, no conspiracy.' 'All turned on premeditation. If none, Rome no accomplice.' Instead he diverts attention by amassing large amounts of documentary evidence concerning the public rejoicing in Rome following news of the massacre, assuming illogically that this is tantamount to implication in the conspiracy. Through the Cardinal of Lorraine he traces the plot back to Gregory XIII at the centre of the web, and the article gives extensive and graphic descriptions of the Pope striking medals, commissioning Vasari to paint frescoes depicting scenes of the massacre, ordering *Te Deums* and in general exhausting 'the modes by which a Pope could manifest delight'.[21]

But the central target is not Gregory XIII nor Catherine de Medici, for by contradictorily shifting his ground Acton moved from political expediency to religious morality and 'the permanent and incurable perversion of moral sense wrought by a distorted piety'. It was his fellow historians, the Catholic apologists, those architects of 'the vast tradition of conventional mendacity', whom he was resolved to destroy. He ended by making a direct connection between the cruelty of the Counter-Reformation spirit and the current fabricators of ultramontanism. 'That which had been defiantly acknowledged and defended required to be ingeniously explained away. The same motive which had justified the murder now prompted the lie.' It was Newman who grasped that far from being disinterested, Acton's history was highly engaged and purposeful, that he was using the past to attack Cardinal Antonelli and the Jesuit clique surrounding Pius IX. Wittily he captured the house style of the *Rambler* (he writes of Simpson, but it could apply equally to Acton): 'He will always be flicking his whips at Bishops, cutting them in tender places, throwing stones at Sacred Congregations and, as he rides along the highroad, discharging peashooters at Cardinals who happen by bad luck to look out of the window.' 'The Massacre of St Bartholomew' was aimed specifically and directly at the forthcoming Vatican Council, and its history was bad because of this ulterior motive. Because history was a hanging matter Acton insisted that it was essential that a man not be hanged on damaged testimony. Here decidedly he fabricated damaging testimony, approached the trial as prosecutor not as judge, presumed guilt in advance in order to hang the innocent.[22]

In the following year at the Vatican Council the historian entered history, helping to mould and not merely to write it. His efforts in mounting opposition to the infallibilists were prodigious: he acted as chief go-between, organizer and strategist, rallying support, attempting to win over the faint-hearted inopportunists, labouring ceaselessly each day before retiring to bed exhausted at four or five each morning. Perhaps it was this draining activity, along with the enervating humidity of a Roman summer, the certain knowledge of being perpetually spied upon, of his letters being opened by the Vatican post office (he resorted to pseudonyms when writing of the chief participants in the drama) and a growing fear of assassination, that partly unhinged him. Lord Odo Russell records a bizarre conversation in Rome that climactic summer, with Acton launching into an extraordinary diatribe against the Church which culminated in the following remarkable words: 'I pray to God that I may live to see the whole of this fabric destroyed, and the Tiber flow with the blood of massacred priests.' 'At which point,' Russell continues, 'Mr Cartwright bound from his chair, and Mrs Craven folded her hands in prayer to supplicate him to stop.' It was, as Manning recalled, no time for rosewater. For at the Council Manning had forcefully maintained that 'Authority must conquer history' and he intended this quite literally, for when Archbishop Guidi of Bologna had imprudently referred in public to the contravention of traditional conciliar unanimity required in matters of faith and morals, he was first held forcibly in his room, then carpeted by the Pope with the words, 'I am the tradition.' It was not just the Council's concentration of spiritual powers in papal hands, its destruction of freedoms within the Church, its wholesale rejection of reform, nor even its explicit rejection of a genuine ecumenicalism which concerned Acton. Even more threatening was its denial of history and its retrospective absolution of all preceding papal abuses which the dogma assumed. With its promulgation, 'the acts of the buried and repented past would come back at once and for ever, with a crushing weight on the Church. Spectres it had taken ages of sorrowful effort to lay would come forth once more.'[23] Because truth as well as liberty was at stake Acton could yield no quarter; as a historian he struggled on behalf of the past, and as a Catholic for the present. There was not a shred of historical authenticity in infallibilist claims and he determined to counter authority with history and expose the Pope as 'the fiend skulking behind the Crucifix'. Because the Council had assented to this culminating act of papal aggression it constituted 'an organized conspiracy to establish a power which would be the most formidable enemy of liberty as well as science throughout the world ... To proclaim the Pope infallible was [the ultramontanes'] compendious security against hostile States and Churches, against human liberty and authority, against disintegrating tolerance and rationalizing science, against error and sin.'[24] Acton failed. Veneration for the Pope, the extensive use of his power and patronage entrenched over an unprecedented tenure of twenty-four years, the fear of schism and the ultimate threat of excommunication were together sufficient to bring inopportunist and minimalist to heel, and those who could not bring themselves to submit fled the city. The dogma at last confirmed that the kingdom of God did indeed lie between Montefiascone and Terracine, and that German science had been roundly defeated by the obscurantism of Italian prelates.

But the crisis did not end there; it moved instead from the public into the private sphere, where the events of 1874 and 1875 were to exert a lasting influence on the historian's writing and character. It all began in February 1874 with the defeat of Gladstone's government over the Irish University bill and his resignation from the leadership of the Liberal Party in the following year. Rendered dangerously inactive, Gladstone had leisure to reflect upon the pernicious obstructionism of the Catholic bishops to his Irish strategy. Other personal factors turned his attention to malign Vaticanism. He had never fully recovered from the devastating defection to Rome of his two closest friends, Hope-Scott and Manning; his beloved sister Helen had also become estranged and converted in 1842. His own attitude towards the Catholic Church was ambivalent: he admired its tradition and its universalism yet deplored its authoritarianism; he yearned for an ecumenicalism centred upon the Anglican *via media*, but this was rendered impossible by the extravagant and distancing claims of the papacy; his own High Church observances were such as to lead to persistent rumours that he himself was a secret convert. In September 1873 an emotional meeting with the excommunicated Döllinger was swiftly followed by news of Lord Ripon's conversion in the same month, all the more sensational given that he was both Lord President of the Council and Grand Master of the English Freemasons. The Gladstonian volcano erupted and three stinging pamphlets followed in which he accused the Vatican Council of denying moral and intellectual freedom, destroying the civil loyalty of every English Catholic, and repudiating 'modern thought and ancient history'.[25]

Acton was appalled. The Cabinet had not been consulted and he feared the recrudescence of a 'no popery' campaign. But most of all he was appalled because Gladstone was merely repeating, lock, stock and barrel, every single argument rehearsed by Acton both publicly and privately before and after the Council. For, in a desperate gamble to involve the powers, he had written Gladstone a number of letters, those of 16 February and 11 March 1870 in particular, stating clearly that papal infallibility was incompatible with civil loyalty. This bid sadly miscalculated Cabinet opinion, and Lord Clarendon and his stepfather were easily able to isolate Gladstone in his urge to intervene by emphasizing the domestic priority of good relations with the Irish bishops. In the light of these repeated claims on Gladstone from the Council Acton had of necessity to concede that *prima facie* Gladstone had a strong case. But while seeming to advance belligerently in the first of his four letters to *The Times*, dated 8 November, Acton was in truth attempting a tactical retreat, an escape from theology to what he hoped was the safer ground of history. In answer to Gladstone he attempted to dissociate the ultramontanists of the Council from the ultramontane spirit of the past, and to insist that exaggerated fears of divided Catholic loyalties neglected 'the infinite subtlety and inconsistency with which men practically elude the yoke of official uniformity in matters of opinion'. Thus, for example, although Pius v had evoked the deposing power, excommunicated Elizabeth I and plotted her assassination, the English Catholic community had in the main remained loyal. But again Acton's strategy miscarried. Gladstone was bewildered, left breathless from trying to keep pace with his friend's astonishing *volte-face*. Manning, shark-like, smelled blood and attacked. Acton's letters not only accused a saint of the Church of planning assassination, but also argued that English Catholics could evade the fullest implications of the recent decrees. He wrote three times demanding a complete statement of orthodoxy. Unsatisfied by all three replies he passed the matter on to Rome in January 1875. Acton swung agonizingly on the hook, expecting excommunication in a matter of months. He had stated in his fourth letter, of 9 December, that to 'imagine that British institutions are secure because ecclesiastical authority may be evaded by those who choose to equivocate, or that conscience can be sheltered by duplicity, would be the part of an idiot'. Yet Acton did precisely this. He pondered the Jansenists' 'respectful silence', Galileo's outward recantation and inward assertion – 'Eppur si muove' ('But it does move') – and in his *Times* letters he analysed the case for Fénelon's (1651–1715) censure of quietism. He re-rehearsed the dilemma he faced in 1864 following the implicit papal censure of the *Rambler* under his editorship, but now the case was altogether different and more perplexing. Then he had resolved the problem of continuing obedience with freedom of thought by voluntarily terminating its publication. Now the matter demanded the full submission of his conscience, and the only alternatives were to yield or to cease to profess his faith. Were public submission and private resistance compatible? he asked. Was it possible to draw a fine line between equivocation and subtlety in response to the iron rule of conformity? Could Archbishop Manning insist upon inward assent as well as outward acquiescence? Suddenly Acton's stark clarity of mind gave way to uncharacteristic vagueness and disingenuousness. The decrees were harmless; they presented him with no problems. He informed Newman of his casual, imperfect knowledge of the Tridentine decrees. He was incurious, loath to master details – this from the historian who had collected voluminous materials on this very subject throughout the 1860s.[26]

Yet it was Newman who saved him at this gravest juncture. Acton's retreat of 1875 reflected his increasing practical isolation within the Church since 1870. He strove at first to sustain the flagging spirits of the minority bishops in his *Sendschreiben* aimed against the 'soul-endangering error' of submission. The letter was instantly placed on the Index. Hefele of Rottenburg and Haynald of Kalosca submitted in 1871, Strossmeyer of Bosnia in 1872. Clifford of Clifton, vociferous enough at the Council, now refused Acton access to his papers by which he hoped to pursue the campaign on behalf of the minority. Connolly of Halifax wrote arguing that further resistance would be schismatic. Kenrick of St Louis, reported to Döllinger earlier that year as standing firm, succumbed on 2 January 1871. It was Kenrick who had written to Acton suggesting that just as the *Essay on the Development of Christian Doctrine* had enabled Newman to enter the Church, so it justified Kenrick's – and by implication, Acton's – remaining in it. That *Essay* was, in Newman's own words, 'an hypothesis to account for a difficulty' which he faced in 1845 during a crisis in his own spiritual life as he teetered on the edge of conversion. The difficulty was one of reconciling the original revelation of the early Christian Fathers with the accretion of dogma which had produced a radically different nineteenth-century Church. Mutability characterized the Church's earthly existence, but the development of doctrine was not one of change and decay but rather,

as he expressed it to Acton in 1862, 'a more intimate appre-
hension, and a more lucid enunciation of the original dogma
... a process by which, under the *magisterium* of the Church,
implicit faith becomes explicit'.[27] Technically this interpretation enabled Acton to justify his remaining in the Church
and submitting on the clear understanding that in the long
run his objections would be reconciled and harmonized by
a divine sifting, and the current ultramontane aberration made
ultimately consistent with the true deposit of faith.

Most secondary authorities, Victor Conzemius, Gertrude
Himmelfarb, E. D. Watt, have exonerated Acton of duplicity
in 1874 and 1875. But judged by his own and not the common
code, this crisis constituted, as Lionel Kochan argues, a self-
betrayal.[28] Certainly Gladstone for one condemned Acton's
equivocations in letters he wrote to Döllinger and Granville.
And Acton himself seems to have expressed unconscious
doubts. A list remains in which he scribbled down at random
some of the infinite varieties of doubtful actions, among which
were 'May one resist the state? Or cashier a king? Or be
husband of two wives? *Or deceive a questioner?*'[29] Manning
remained unsatisfied by Acton's equivocal replies to his
inquisition but drew satisfaction from having silenced the
wise man of German scholarship. Acton had on a number
of occasions expressed the clear opinion that anyone who
attempted to assert the fallibility of the Pope would have in
the last resort to face excommunication, but when that
moment arose he could not bear to suffer the consequences.
Instead, encouraged by Döllinger's insistence that no one
should voluntarily sever their ties with the Church, he resorted
to Newman's *Essay*, whose advantage lay in its infinite elasticity, its capacity to mitigate, justify and palliate. For Acton
its appeal lay in its ability to sustain not that which was and
is, but rather that which may be. Newman had argued that
in some cases heresy was merely orthodoxy's advanced guard.
Acton appreciated that the *Essay* could serve not only to con-
secrate the present dispensation but also to hold out the prospect of consistency between heterodox deviation and Church

doctrine in the future. This let him off the hook, but only at the cost of temporarily abandoning a system of absolute for relative ethics. He kept well away from Newman's domain of doctrinal theology in 1874, but the whole thrust of his writing up till then had been a constant denial that dogma and ethics were separable. Now he attempted to distinguish between the ultramontane spirit in history and its current manifestation at the Council, between theology and politics, whereas before the 'wavy line' had confirmed that both were inextricably bound together in one single ethical system of ends and means. It was with the understanding that Newman's *Essay* provided a refuge for opportunism that he placed its author among those other inopportunists – Rosmini, Lacordaire, Hefele, Falloux – who together reflected 'the mere adjustment of religious history to the ethics of Whiggism'.[30] Like condemned criminals they all hoped to escape punishment by a quibble. But had not Acton too got off on a quibble? Had he not desperately grasped at inopportunism in order successfully to escape excommunication?

Two psychological consequences followed from this. One was the arresting of self-doubt and the salving of painful memories by means of calculated amnesia. When Purcell's *Life of Manning* appeared in 1895 Acton was shocked to reread his forgotten correspondence with Gladstone from the Council twenty-five years previously. Shaken by public exposure, he wrote to Gladstone saying he could remember having written only two letters when in fact he had written over twenty. The other, more corroding consequence served to reinforce a characteristic already present but which left a deeper imprint on the historian's writings after 1874. This was a deep sense of guilt, a stifled sense of self-betrayal issuing in a profound self-hatred which was only assuaged by subconscious transference to other objects. Thus Newman who had saved him became that 'splendid sophist', the projected object which deflected self-loathing and which psychologically compensated for the refusal to recognize that perhaps he, Acton, was the true sophist. Newman had incurred this condemnation merely by assisting in Acton's strategy of self-deception. Thereafter the hardening of his intellectual arteries and the stultification of his emotional empathy increased. The obsessive fulminations against all equivocators, all evaders of justice, became the rage of Caliban upon glimpsing himself in a looking-glass. This led, most unforgivably, to his intellectual estrangement from Döllinger after 1883. His offence? Döllinger had written a brief, generous introduction to an article by Charlotte Blennerhassett on Acton's old teacher, Dupanloup, after Charlotte had felt unable to use a harsher biographical memoir provided by Acton. Dupanloup had written a moderating gloss on the *Syllabus of Errors* and had been an inopportunist at the Council, and Acton never forgave Döllinger for this minor act of treachery. Acton's biographers have all stressed the endless self-dramatizing confessions of alienation to Döllinger after 1879, concentrating exclusively upon the revelation of crippling ethical isolation. But in doing so they tend to forget that while the kindly priest suffered excommunication in 1871 the self-pitying layman was spared four years later.

4   The Liberal

After their intellectual breach Acton spoke of having lost the key to Döllinger's mind, that further conversation was to cease on earth. The master dismissed his pupil's remorseless severity as 'immature eagerness' and 'youthful rashness', and Acton retreated, heavy-hearted, into 'the loneliness of self-government'. But regular personal contact continued until Döllinger's death in 1890. A photograph survives of a group taken in the grounds of Tegernsee, Acton's lakeside home in Bavaria, in 1879. To the left, in deferential background, Mary and Herbert, two of Gladstone's children. Between Mr and Mrs Gladstone sits an abstracted, gloomy little girl, clad in dark stockings and boots and an inordinately large white bonnet, seemingly unaware of the illustrious company clustered around her. Then the eighty-year-old Döllinger, small and rather shrivelled in appearance, but with a face bright and alert. At the extreme right and some short distance from the others, Acton thick-set and heavy with immense beard, receding hair and large forehead, that 'cold white cliff' as Henry Scott Holland called it, a visible symbol – as contemporaries invariably commented – of the vast knowledge that lay within. Gladstone found relief in light French comedies and long heavy theological discussions with the Professor while rowing on the lake or climbing its surrounding Alpine foothills. Döllinger, increasingly deaf and insomniac, would lie awake for hours memorizing book after book of the *Odyssey* by heart. Acton would retreat to his library to read and return to the endless process of 'sticking eternal bits of paper into innumerable books, and putting larger papers into black boxes'.[1] His sense of intellectual alienation grew: he spoke of his 'elaborate detachment, the unamiable isolation,

the dread of personal influences', and among his papers after
his death a portrait was found, perhaps transcribed from a
passage which held peculiar relevance for him.

> He was reserved about himself, and gave no explanations,
> so that he was constantly misunderstood, and there was
> a sense of failure, of disappointment, of perplexity about
> him... But I doubted whether all this was not artificial,
> – a contrivance to satisfy the pride of intellect and establish
> a cold superiority. In time I discovered that it was the perfec-
> tion of a developed character. He had disciplined his soul
> with such wisdom and energy as to make it the obedient
> and spontaneous instrument of God's will, and he moved
> in an orbit of thoughts beyond our reach.[2]

But too much can be made of Acton's over-dramatization
of his intellectual history, for other, possibly more compelling,
factors besides the complex compound of humility and pride
contributed to his sense of isolation. Some were eminently
practical. There was a substantial loss of income in the middle
years: returns from his 6,000-acre Shropshire estates fell during the long agricultural depression beginning in the 1870s;
his stepfather's ironworks foundered and only a major salvag-
ing operation saved Granville from bankruptcy and kept his
political career afloat. Financial retrenchments became necessary. The ancestral Dalberg castle and estates at Herrnsheim
were finally sold off in 1883, Aldenham was sublet, and Acton
divided his time increasingly between Tegernsee and a villa
he bought in Cannes. Shortage of money forced him to solicit
humiliatingly for salaried political posts, but at least his
relative poverty gave him an excuse to terminate the post
of chaplain at Aldenham. In this matter his run of bad luck
had continued, for Brande Morris had been replaced by Father
David Williams, who was given to snooping through his master's library in his absence and, shocked to find a parody
of Baring Gould's *Lives of the Saints*, took it upon himself
to report the discovery to his bishop.

Domestically Acton was shattered by the infant deaths of
two of his children; then he worried himself with the raising
and education of the remaining four. More obscure and incalculable were his relations with his wife. Scattered through
his papers are intimations of pain and unhappiness, of an
implacable husband and a suffering wife, with scraps of a
torn-up letter by Marie pleading, 'For the love of your children
don't be pitiless.'[3] He had an emotional need for the sympathy
and support of intelligent women, as his letters to Charlotte
Blennerhassett, Mary Drew and his daughter Mamy attest.
He enjoyed male company too. He was no scholarly recluse,
but belonged to all the right clubs – Brooks's, the Athenaeum,
the Travellers', the Grillion – and that immoderate diner-out,
Lord Mountstuart Grant Duff, records having met him in
company twelve times in 1893 alone. He could dazzle in after-
dinner company, yet as suddenly freeze and his cold blue eyes
silence the table in seconds. For there was a Jansenist rigour
in his make-up, an austere dislike of sensuous indulgence and
epicurean enjoyment, and the reader will search his writings
in vain for a description of food or wine, the beauties of
a landscape, or for reflections upon art or music. He depre-
cated the Renaissance precisely because a large part of its
learning was transmuted into aesthetics, and found the joyless
ascetic combat of the Reformation and Counter-Reformation
more congenial to his tastes. His intellectual ingenuity was
no substitute for an instinctive lack of political *nous*. Too
clever by half, he frequently miscalculated by endowing his
opponents with a greater complexity than they possessed and
consequently lost by playing a game quite different from their
own. His moral rectitude and principled stands made it difficult to adjust to the pliant bargaining and subtle shifts of
political alliance and burdened him with an unenviable reputation for clumsy flat-footedness. Thus, when he demanded
Cabinet intervention against the Vatican Council, his stepfather, 'Pussy' Granville, coolly and correctly pointed out that
it was not the duty of Protestant Britain to expel the Pope
from Rome and that no one took papal encyclicals very

seriously anyhow. Part of the trouble was that while Acton yearned for public office his temperament would not allow him publicly to avow such ambition or to play openly according to the accepted ground rules of political life, which he characterized as standing somewhere between Boccaccio and Brantôme.

Given all this it is not surprising that an unfortunate element of farce is inseparable from an account of his political career. On the look-out for a suitable seat he considered Clare before Carlow offered itself in 1859. Even by Irish standards Carlow was a thoroughly rotten borough run by the local priest, Father James Maher, who could easily manage the 236 voters in a constituency of 9,000 souls. The twenty-five-year-old candidate treated his electors with a truly Burkean disdain, issuing neither a programme nor an electoral address, and absenting himself from the election itself when dragoons had to be called in to quell a riot between rival Catholic factions. He turned up just once for a banquet to celebrate his election and thereafter entirely neglected the interests of the citizens he represented and the whig cause generally. He sat on three parliamentary commissions, spoke three times in the House and voted in only twenty-seven divisions during seven years. Given such a lamentable performance it is not surprising that the admittedly hostile *Carlow Sentinel* accused its MP of being 'as much acquainted with the interests of a commercial community as a resident in Nova Scotia entitled to vote by proxy' and his constituents started looking elsewhere.[4] In 1865 he stood for his local Bridgnorth constituency, scraping in by a single vote, but the opposition called for a recount and an investigation. Acton responded by denying that he had tempted the integrity of the electorate, but the commission found evidence of corruption by his agents and he was unseated in 1866. He tried once more in 1868, was unsuccessful, and Gladstone mercifully came to his rescue by elevating him to the Lords in 1869. Thereafter he served the Liberal cause loyally and not unnaturally expected some reward for his efforts. These expectations climaxed in 1892 with the formation of Gladstone's fourth and final ministry. Acton made one last effort to secure the Munich embassy he had long coveted, going so far as to suggest a knighthood for Drummond, his chief competitor, to impress his American wife and secure her acquiescent exile to Latin America. This failed, but the far more dazzling prospect of a Cabinet post had been absent-mindedly dangled before him by Gladstone at Braemar in July 1892. It was a difficult and confused time, for Acton was involved in the delicate task of securing the co-operation of Lord Rosebery at a time when that reluctant Liberal leader was suffering severe depression following the death of his wife. It was a measure of Gladstone's lack of political grip that he could have made so startling and unauthorized an offer, and when news of it reached the Cabinet it sparked off a revolt led by Lord Spencer. Acton was simply not of Cabinet standing. So this offer too was hurriedly dropped, and in desperation Acton sent off a number of begging letters via Mary Drew during the last unseemly scramble for salaried patronage. During August he was offered the 'incongruous' post of Captain of the Yeomen of the Guard, which involved his getting togged up in uniform and whose title suggested something out of the D'Oyly Carte repertoire; he gratefully clutched at the alternative offer of Lord in Waiting, which at least had the advantage of allowing him access to the royal library at Windsor.[5]

Acton's increased preoccupation with politics from the 1870s onwards, his progression from liberal Catholic to Liberal, was easily accomplished. Throughout the 1860s he fought the advance of spiritual authoritarianism: in 1870 he failed to halt it and in 1874 the struggle proved to be even more perilous than he had at first imagined. But his central spiritual concerns were not abandoned, merely channelled and secularized in an attempt to transform and redeem the political world through party. All that was required was a simple conversion of spiritual opportunism into whig expediency, religious ultramontanism into political toryism and the transformation of the 'minority' bishops into Gladstonians. This politicization can be traced in his journalism, from the predominantly theological preoccupations of the *Rambler* to the overtly Liberal politics of the *Chronicle*, whose role, as Acton described it to Gladstone, was to serve as 'a literary organ for the renovated party'. The transformation was complete: 'Have you not discovered,' he wrote to Mary Drew, 'have I never betrayed, what a narrow doctrinaire I am, under a thin disguise of levity?... Politics come nearer religion with me, a party is more like a church, error more like heresy, prejudice more like sin, than I find it to be with better men.'[6] This made for a rather peculiar species of political animal. If political, like religious truth, was absolute and indivisible, then Britain's two-party adversarial politics was nothing less than institutionalized obstructionalism and a grave concession to false political relativism. He had rejected this party orthodoxy as early as 1863. 'Our political system is founded on definite principles, not on compact or compromise. Every compromise marks an imperfect realization of principle – a surrender of right to interest or force. The constitution stands by its own strength, not by the equal strain of opposite forces.' It followed that, because the Liberal party possessed an absolute monopoly of legitimacy, toryism was not an alternative that could be recognized or tolerated, but an opposition to be obliterated or absorbed. His repeated assertion that a better argument had always to be made for the enemy than the enemy could itself make, was not a concession but rather, because of its predictable outcome, a foreclosing of debate, a recognition that the opposition had no real case to argue at all. Consequently he was astonished when Sir Henry Sumner Maine failed to appreciate that the term 'tory' on Acton's lips was a term of severe reproach. The practical consequence of this inflexibility was to perpetuate and intensify the abhorred party system, but it did have the singular advantage of identifying the chief enemy of the renovated party, which was calculated opportunism. Now Burke was to be hanged alongside Robespierre because he 'loved to evade the arbitration of principle'.[7]

If Acton's political principles were merely an aspect of his
religious beliefs it was because he never ceased to believe that
Christ's coming had redeemed the political as well as the spiritual world. The gospel message had humbled the supremacy
of rank and wealth and forbidden the state to encroach on
God's domain, 'by teaching man to love his neighbour as
himself; by promoting the sense of equality; by condemning
the pride of race, which was a stimulus of conquest, and the
doctrine of separate descent, which formed the philosopher's
defence of slavery'. The ancients had advanced the cause of
liberty but their writings were but faint pagan premonitions
of the doctrine of the sovereign conscience. That doctrine
correspondingly required the precondition of political liberty,
for just as absolute government contradicted the divine law
so 'Christianity without liberality will not take us far towards
heaven,' and liberty advanced by 'sanctifying freedom and
consecrating it to God'.[8] A purely secular conception of
liberty, a definition of freedom devoid of divine sanction, was
inconceivable, and every species of political agnosticism
anathema to him. Good Catholic that he was, he interpreted
the Reformation as contributing ultimately to Machiavelli's
separation of ethics from politics, and in the last quarter of
the nineteenth century he continued to dismiss Bentham's and
Mill's attempts to advance a wholly humanistic progressivism.
Even the fairly innocuous John Morley, referred to as 'Pris-
cilla' by his Cabinet colleagues, was spoken of in the oddest
manner as being full of 'Jacobinical possibilities' because he
had made a special study of eighteenth-century French sceptics
and nineteenth-century positivists: 'As there are, for him, no
rights of God, there are no rights of man – the consequence,
on earth, of obligation in heaven.' Similarly the greatest com-
pliment Acton could pay George Eliot was that her ethical
teaching 'was the highest within the resources to which
Atheism is restricted'.[9]

The Catholic Acton still looked to voluntaristic universalism as the model for an ideal state. Whereas before Mazzini
and Cavour had advanced Italian nationalism at the expense

of the Church, now, infinitely more powerful and aggressive, that same force of nationalism, concentrated in the hands of Bismarck and theoreticians like Treitschke, was attempting to destroy German Catholicism through the oppressive legislation of the *Kulturkampf*. The historian who wrote a history devoid of frontiers and the liberal who opposed all concentrated powers continued to identify the nation-state as the chief obstacle to universal progress. 'The process of civilization,' he insisted, 'depends on transcending Nationality,' for 'patriotism cannot absolve a man from his duty to mankind.' The only choice was between freedom or the sacrifice of freedom to power. 'The nations aim at power, and the world at freedom,' and a 'generous spirit prefers that his country should be poor, and weak, and of no account, but free rather than powerful, prosperous and enslaved.' Far better to be a citizen of the humble commonwealth of Switzerland than the 'superb autocracy' of Russia. Far better to live within a diverse, tolerant society, a society which did not resent or fear the rich complexity of life, than under one of crushing conformity. His plea against majoritarian tyranny was as eloquent in his lectures on freedom in 1877 as those delivered to the same Bridgnorth audience in 1866.

It is bad to be oppressed by a minority, but is worse to be oppressed by a majority. For there is a reserve of latent power in the masses which, if it is called into play, the minority can seldom resist. But from the absolute will of an entire people there is no appeal, no redemption, no refuge but treason.[10]

Like Mill and every other liberal theoretician of his day Acton feared the logical consequences of democratic principles and sought by a variety of mechanical methods – proportional representation, plural voting, a strengthened House of Lords – to muffle and restrict universal suffrage. And because he shared the common nightmare of the drowning of wisdom in numbers, the unleashing of ignorance, prejudice and passion, he appealed to liberty not as a consummation but as a restraint on democracy. But unlike most of his contemporaries he did not employ Tocqueville's insights into mass democracy for purely conservative ends, because he recognized that powerful minorities also constituted a threat and appreciated that despite all its risks participatory politics remained an essential precondition of liberty. Now, as in 1870, he concentrated his attack on the monstrous abuses of the powerful and on the intellectual apologists who sustained them: Droysen's historical deification of Prussian militarism; Gobineau's racial doctrines which denied free will, responsibility and guilt and justified European imperialism. His assault on British jingoism ('We despised conquest, but annexed with the greed of Russia') earned him censure for 'want of national fibre' in his *Times* obituary. His humanity and compassion made him keenly alive to the 'glory' of war, 'the effects of wounds... the cannon wheels crashing over the bones of the wounded... the havoc wrought by a piece of shell tearing through the living trunk... the scenes in the hospitals, the ruined homes, the devastation'.[11] As an aristocrat he had not a shred of reverence or deference. Because liberalism was classless he rejected the conservative theory of rule by vested interest just as he dismissed the Marxist equivalent of rule by the proletarian dictatorship. It was not a question of one particular class being unfit to govern but rather that every class was equally unfitted.

It was the concentration of political and economic power in the hands of one class and the demoralizing, soul-destroying consequences of poverty, not Marx's material dialectic, which led him to recommend *Das Kapital* to Gladstone. At a time when Spencer and Maine were advancing the extreme laissez-faire case against any regression into socialism, Acton was arguing for a liberalism which went beyond negative non-intervention to a positive state 'where the public is subject to no restrictions but those of which it feels the advantage'.[12] He discerned two distinct traditions stemming from Adam Smith's economic liberalism. The first, the principle of free contract between labour and capital, had initially advanced the politics of freedom, while the second, the theory of labour as source of all wealth, had laid the foundations of socialism and the revolutionary threat of levelling expropriation. But the harshness of capitalism and its perpetuation of privilege – its granting of seconds, arms and ammunition to only one side in life's duel – led him to advocate a compromise alternative of sharing political power as a safer preliminary to fairer economic redistribution.

This tone of mild radicalism in his later writing, the typical stylistic indulgence in hyperbole and superlative, the pose as prophetic seer, were among the many advantages Acton derived from his close friendship with Gladstone. For Acton not only gained privileged access, he gained access secure in the knowledge that the Prime Minister would translate only the most practical consequences of his theorizing into policy. When, in February 1885, he was once more dissuading Gladstone from thoughts of retirement, Acton's appeal to the stability and continuity which the GOM bestowed upon his party and the state against 'the outer signs of change, to bridge the apparent chasm' applied equally to the stability and continuity of Acton's privileged role as adviser.[13] Emotionally too he gained, for Gladstone, twenty years older, began to replace Döllinger as father figure, though now Acton had come of age and in certain areas dominated the partnership.

Acton had not always been an admirer. In 1860 he spoke of Gladstone's 'utmost intellectual duplicity' and his 'fatal instability of purpose'. The friendship developed only gradually and was always slightly ticklish. There was the matter of Gladstone's close political relationship with Granville and the possible accusation of nepotism and, as Acton's epistolary intimacy with Mary Gladstone grew, the embarrassing question of what letters – the blush-making generosity of his estimate of Gladstone in 1880 for example? – the daughter passed on to her father. Support for the confederacy and the disestablishment of the Irish Church brought them closer politically in the 1860s, and despite the contretemps of 1874, it was increasingly gossiped abroad – Wilfred Ward picked it up from Sir Rowland Blennerhassett – that Acton intended to rule England through Gladstone. Matthew Arnold spoke of the seminal influence the historian exercised over the Prime Minister; Sir Edward Hamilton, Gladstone's secretary, repeated it endlessly, and Acton told his daughter Mamy that Gladstone had told him that he trusted him more entirely than any other man. Even Cardinal Manning encouraged this estimate, though from a critical angle. 'Gladstone's geese were always swans. His friendship always blinds him. Time was when I had the benefit of his illusions. When this turned, Acton was the man made to his hand. He was a Catholic, learned in literature, of a German industry, cold, self-confident, supercilious towards opponents, a disciple of Döllinger, and predisposed against me.'[14]

Until recently historians of the school of high politics have played down the possibility that Gladstone had any motives other than political and tactical ones. Reacting against the hagiography of John Morley and J. L. Hammond, they observed a calculating master of parliamentary art, a consummate strategist advancing the joint cause of personal and party fortune. If this was so then any extra-parliamentary influence such as Acton's doctrinaire ideology was peripheral at best, verbiage to be converted into hard practical advantage. The trouble with this interpretation is that it fails to do justice to the bewildering complexity of Gladstone, reducing him to one dimension and artificially separating the political from the religious being. Only now, assisted by the publication of the diaries, is a fresh recomposition of his theological politics emerging, which attempts to put the extraordinary man together again. Extraordinary because, often against his own wishes, Gladstone was an adroit politician, a determined inegalitarian but a populist demagogue too, a scholar of sorts and, above all, a man of profound religious conviction. If, as A. V. Dicey said, the trouble with Gladstone was that he was not Gladstonian, that he eluded the simplifications of friend and foe alike, then it is possible to reinstate Acton to a degree of influence. If Gladstone's confession to Acton that 'It is a great and high call to walk by faith and not by sight' is humbug in Stracheyesque terms, then it was a humbug which bound them together and gave the historian a degree of leverage over the politician which can be partly measured by the constant pleas by Gladstone for Acton to end his self-imposed exile on the Riviera.[15]

What the correspondence with Gladstone directly and with Mary indirectly demonstrates is that Acton's role was inspirational rather than practical, ideological more than political, his task to confirm and support rather than initiate, and to pitch each construction of policy at the highest possible level. More especially it was a question of keeping the PM up to the mark while the providential task remained incomplete: 'he is too willing to take facts in a favourable light,' he wrote via Mary, 'and a little slow to accept what is adverse to the cause' (18 June 1886). 'There is a want of vigour in the management of his colleagues, and a tendency to postpone things' (29 March 1893). There was much scholarly talk when the historian was asked to help the lame dog over the stile, but pre-eminently there was spiritual counsel and solace. At times theology separated them, as when an unseemly and prolix struggle for the soul of Gladstone's sister Helen followed upon her death in 1880, each party claiming her for their own Church. But in general their common religiosity held them together in the face of advancing unbelief and a decline in transcendentalism. Everywhere he turned Gladstone observed fresh quack remedies such as the empty theism of Mrs Humphry Ward's *Robert Elsmere* ('the Gospels and the New Testament must have much else besides miracle torn out of them in order to get us down to the *Caput Mortuum* of Elgood Street' where our hero dies exhausted from his mission-house labours), or the propagation of positivism ('I cannot think the Ethical order safe in their hands. There are shocking things in Comte').[16]

Yet behind this haze of contemplation there was calculation: the opportunity was too tempting, the desire to play philosopher king too strong. Aware of the baleful conjunction of princes and professors in history, ever suspicious of power's corroding influence, Acton exempted himself and remained blithely unaware of his own temptations. Yet he held Gladstone's 'lofty unfitness to deal with sordid motives' to be his chief political flaw. He did not scruple in 1885 to persist in urging the case of the High Church Liddon for the London see: the PM had authority to do what he liked, ignore common cavil, exert patronage for the supreme motive. A balanced ticket offered by the 'providential opportunity' of a vacant Lincoln see helped clinch his proposal. Again in 1891, when there was ample evidence that female suffrage would further the clerical tory cause, he pressed the interest of party over the protection of man's victims.[17]

'The Madonna of the Future' (Acton's ironic title for his unwritten history) was conceived in stirring days. Once more a regenerative spirit seemed abroad in the land and, as in 1857 on his return to England from Germany, everything once more seemed possible. In 1875 Gladstone had retired from high office, determined upon a final interval of rest between parliament and the grave. But a year later he was fulminating in print against the Bulgarian atrocities and in his Midlothian campaign of 1879–80 riding the spontaneous unleashing of Victorian moral outrage against the calculating amorality of Disraeli's foreign policy. In this feverish atmosphere Acton delivered his two lectures on 'The History of Freedom' (February and May 1877) and wrote his review of Erskine May's *Democracy in Europe* (1878), setting out the forthcoming Gladstonian agenda. All three show the historian once more enmeshed in the web of current controversy, his history determined by contemporary concerns, and a vision of the past evoked to make sense of the present. While no bland celebration of late-Victorian values, it did tether the future of progress firmly to a Gladstonian *via media*.

Since the martyrdom of Socrates and the writings of Plato, the need for restraints on pure democracy had been recognized. Aware of the evil of investing control in any one section of society, Solon had wisely distributed power, making each Athenian citizen guardian of his own interests. He went further, for in distinguishing between legislative decrees and a fundamental constitution by which those decrees were to be judged, he entrenched the rule of law above and beyond the arbitrary changes of opinion and made the people trustees and not masters of the state. Much later this dual system of laws was replicated by the founding fathers in an American constitution which embodied and advanced their revolutionary principles. The French revolutionaries were inspired in turn by the American spirit of 1776 but failed to grasp or implement the concomitant stabilizing mechanism of its 1787 constitution. France's initial hopes of freedom were destroyed by her passion for equality, and the revolution failed. Bestowing all the inherited plenitude of the Crown's despotism upon the sovereign masses, the Jacobins rejected every middle-class Girondist attempt at restraint, and the varied solutions of a constitutional monarchy, a disestablished Church and decentralized government fell before the inexorable logic of pure revolutionary theory. Marat argued that self-preservation absolved the poor of their contractual obligations and instigated the radical politics of expropriation which inspired the revolutions of 1848 and advanced the cause of socialism, 'the infirmity that attends mature democracies'.[18]

Yet on the eve of Gladstonian revolution, Acton was more concerned with the earlier revolution that had succeeded – the American Revolution – in the hope that it might provide a safe passage through the current political shoals. The American example revealed that revolutions could be just and that democracies could, in certain circumstances, be safe. Its federal constitution checked and divided power at every level; its Senate counter-balanced the weight of numbers and its Supreme Court guarded the fundamental law against any infringements or abuse of power. Its appeal lay in its ingenious reconciliation of democracy, liberty and equality. Its mechanism was 'the one immortal tribute of America to political science' for it embodied 'democracy in its highest perfection,

armed and vigilant... against its own weakness and excess',
and consolidated 'the protectorate of minorities, and the con-
secration of self-government'.[19] It offered a remedy to union-
ism, nationalism and every form of powerful concentration,
and in its flexibility, its political ecumenicalism, it was capable
of limitless extension. Thus under the pretext of history Acton
foreshadowed the federalism of Irish Home Rule and its
distribution of sovereignty between Westminster and Dublin.
Skilfully he added the past to the swelling number of Midlothian constituents and implicitly denied the counter-claims
of Chamberlain and the radical wing to the democratic future
based on a caucus, a referendum and a popular party programme. His history reaffirmed the rule of the mandarin élite,
the parliamentarian over the wire-puller, the ideologue over
the party organization, the moral mission over major social
reform. Simultaneously he detached the complacent whig
rump from the body of Gladstonians who, like Solon and
America's founding fathers, pursued the doctrine of the higher
law of conscience. Here most vitally Acton took possession
of the high moral ground, claiming it for 'the age of conversion
and compassion, of increased susceptibility in the national
conscience, of a deepened sense of right and wrong, of much
that, in the eye of rivalry, is sentiment, emotion, idealism,
and imbecility'. That rival, that obstacle to the history of freedom, was Beaconsfieldism which 'bargained with diseased
appetites', exploited popular jingo prejudice and debauched
the moral integrity of the state.[20]

Temporarily Acton's prophecy came true. Gladstone was
returned with an overwhelming majority in the election of
1880 and Ireland began to dominate the agenda. Faced with
relentless opposition, Acton conceived that the only solution
to holding power was to lose it, much as the Liberal solution
to the problem of holding power in Ireland was to give it
away. Throughout the Home Rule crisis Acton measured success in terms of defeat ('it is with a mind prepared for failure
and even disaster that I persist in urging the measure';
'Remember, it will break up the Liberal Party'), failure as

evidence of the absolute righteousness of the cause. Following Morley's denial, he could claim to be the chief ideological instigator of Home Rule. Any number of pragmatic considerations edged Gladstone in this direction: the failure of coercion, the third Reform Bill which admitted eighty-six Irish nationalist MPs into Parliament bent on disrupting procedure, the need once more to unite an endemically fragmented party around a cause sufficient to assuage the Victorian appetite for uplifting crusades, to halt the advance of Chamberlain and head off radical social welfare issues at home, to choke off the possibility of a centralist coalition – all these and others Acton, the alchemist, changed from base metal into gold. In 1886 Ireland was the chosen testing ground of liberal ideology, Gladstone the prime implementer, Acton the high priest and the Reform Bill of 1885 its prelude, 'the advent to power of principles, the commencement of disinterested policy'.[21]

As in the 1860s Acton relished conflict with the enemy. Now the political ultras were Froude, Lecky, Dicey, Salisbury, Fitzjames Stephen and Maine. These unionist apologists argued among themselves. Dicey and Lecky deplored Froude's repressive Cromwellian approach to Ireland. Lecky dispersed his shot by firing at Gladstone in his *Democracy and Liberty* of 1896 and at Froude in his *History of Ireland in the Eighteenth Century* of 1892 because both rejected his solution of rule by a native Anglo-Irish élite. But the conviction that the rule of law in the United Kingdom and throughout the empire required a concentration of powers in the form of absolute parliamentary sovereignty, and a common authoritarian temperament nurtured by British rule in India, held this disparate group together. 'Maine's nature', for example, was 'to exercise power, and to find good reasons for adopted policy'. The theoretical speculations of his *Popular Government* were in reality a sustained assault on Gladstonism. Acton had written eight pages of criticism of this 'Manual of Unacknowledged Conservatism' in proof. Maine not only ignored his every point but specifically requested Acton not to review the book when it appeared in 1885. But the minority – Acton, Bryce,

Morley – were no more disinterested. Gladstone commissioned Bryce to write his huge *American Commonwealth* (1888) on the efficacy of federalism, in order to refute A.V. Dicey's unionist *Law of the Constitution* (1885). History was ransacked indiscriminately for confirmatory material. In April 1886 Bryce wrote despairingly to Acton, 'Croatia and Hungary don't get on at all – their case seems nearest to my scheme, so that is unlucky.' Gladstone took to reading Burke on the eve of Home Rule. Burke's liberalism towards America had failed him over Ireland. Acton now pressed the government forward beyond whig compromise to liberal principle, for 'To admit the American principle was to revolutionize Ireland.'[22]

Revolution had been understood as a criminal usurpation by the young Acton; the purpose of the state was to construct upon the model of the supreme artificer, not to tear down. Revolutions were 'a malady, a frenzy, an interruption of the nation's growth, sometimes fatal to its existence, often to its independence' and ultimately conservative because, with the inevitable counter-revolutionary reaction which followed, genuine reform was prevented. The revolution which destroyed Louis XVI and Necker terminated in the rule of Louis XVIII and Fouché.[23] His maturer understanding of revolution was compounded of a mixture of political, historical and personal motives. Politically the Gladstonian revolution had failed. Hopes of liberalizing the empire had foundered in Egypt and the authoritarian rule of the proconsuls continued. In 1886 and again in 1893 Home Rule was rejected, and while this served to purify the Liberal Party it also cast them into the political desert, the great task unaccomplished. Consequently the easy optimism and moderation of the 1870s gave way to an even greater emphasis on the need for and justness of the revolutionary act just as the successful completion of Gladstonian reform receded in the 1880s and 1890s.

Acton's hopes of a historical revolution had also largely failed. The *History of Freedom* was to have been a manifesto challenging historical orthodoxy. In England Sir Henry

Sumner Maine had pioneered the application of historical method to the field of jurisprudence in his *Ancient Law* of 1861 and, given that much of his field-work was in India, he arrived at the unsurprising conclusion that in legal history habit and custom predominated; that innovation was not only exceptional but usually vain and self-defeating too. This polemicist, who had attacked Gladstone's reform of the Irish land laws, had begun by challenging Bentham's analytical *a priori* jurisprudence and its attempt to subject England's archaic legal system to the rigorous test of reason and the utilitarian calculus. Throwing the entire weight of sluggish history into the balance, Maine suggested that radical change was not only ahistorical but unscientific. Acton was deeply concerned, for this new orthodoxy saturated the writings of most of his fellow historians such as E.A. Freeman, Goldwin Smith, Stubbs and Bryce. The school's emphasis on organic unity and continuity, on the innocuous, uninterrupted enlargement of freedoms, was suspiciously akin to the ultramontane deification of the status quo: that which was, was right. Its stress on tangible institutions and edicts, what Acton called 'ethical materialism' and 'organic constitutionalism', exerted a stultifying, deadening pull on historical writing. He believed that formal institutional history was deceptive and illusory. Without an understanding of the ideas which dictated laws or the spirit which informed structures the empty shell could remain long after the substance had fled. Conventional history 'proved', for example, that indirect elections and a restricted suffrage were inherently conservative, yet all the French revolutionary assemblies were elected indirectly, and a limited suffrage of 90,000 did not prevent the overthrow of Charles x in 1830. The modish adoption of Darwinian metaphors, the concept of a genetic 'seed' transmitting and determining all future growth, imposed a straitjacket on history. Human destiny was programmed much as the inevitable fate of the sunflower seed was to grow into a sunflower. The deterministic replaced free will, inevitability precluded a history of infinite possibilities, mere survival was everything, and habit, custom and

tradition were praised, just as the flourishing weed was preserved. The method was conformist, for a state was deemed
successful only insofar as it perpetuated those peculiar characteristics developed in the past and failed inasmuch as it
deviated from them. With its racial overtones and its theories
of advance through retrogression, of historians attempting
to reach back to the earliest, purest springs of the race, 'historical biology' was profoundly anti-intellectual. To trace the free
institutions of America and Australia back to the primal Teutonic forests was dismissed by Acton as one of the 'desperate
enterprises of historical science'.[24] He did not share the late-
Victorian nostalgia for the ancestral wisdom of barbarians
feeding swine on Hercynian acorns.

His spirited attempts to reverse the assumptions of this
school were, finally, motivated by the need to vindicate a
private history. After his initial subordination to Catholic
apologetic his intellectual growth had been characterized by
violent leaps forward, the consequence of relentless questioning and passionate opposition to authority. He believed that
a true liberal could entertain no reverence for the past, but
should rather destroy great men and established reputations
from a position of resolute independence, should be forever
'on his guard against every tradition and every authority...
following his own conscience into isolation'.[25] History was
an iconoclast, not a teacher of reverence. His own history
of relentless exposure was projected into a historical vocation
which was, at the same time, a source of self-revelation. It
was a discipline which demanded persistent reappraisal and
equally persistent destruction. It led to a history which broke
irreparably with the continuities of custom and habit and
which pivoted instead on revolutionary discontinuities. This
was, in part, the inevitable result of his assigning a pre-eminent
role to ideas over institutions, and to mind over matter. One
innovative idea of, say, Luther or Galileo could, at a stroke,
destroy the entire fabric of the established order and the
presuppositions on which that order was based. The revolutionary potential of speculation was limitless, subversive,

universal in its consequences, exerting an irresistible and irreversible impact. Galileo might recant, but his advances in astronomy could never be destroyed nor his wholly new perception of man's place in the universe be undone. Thus modern history began with 'the advent of the reign of general ideas which we call the Revolution . . . Unheralded, it founded a new order of things, under a law of innovation, sapping the ancient reign of continuity.' This incalculable breach was wrought by Columbus, Machiavelli, Erasmus, Luther, Copernicus. 'It was an awakening of new life; the world revolved in a different orbit, determined by influences unknown before.' Once begun, this perpetual process of discarding and renewal, or breaking and remaking, accelerated and could not be halted. Acton's theory of revolution was a consequence also of his ethical interpretation of history, for revolution was rooted in the knowledge of good and evil, of justice and injustice. Since Plato in his *Republic* had judged the world by the standards of heaven, intellectual idealism had become the source of universal disruption. Revolution was the secular equivalent of spiritual revelation and a prelude to redemption and atonement. Duty to God and the dictates of conscience were doctrines 'laden with storm and havoc' and constituted 'the indestructible soul of Revolution'.[26]

When he spoke in his inaugural lecture at Cambridge of the revolutionist annulling the historian or, in his manuscript notes, 'What was the Revolution? The defeat of History. History dethroned,' he meant, quite literally, that revolutions destroyed the materials out of which history was written; that Condorcet, for example, wished to burn all the records of the French past in order that the reign of the yellow parchment might yield to the light of pure reason. He meant also that the underlying purpose of revolution was to destroy history, that the revolutionary act initially required a purging and purifying before it could embark afresh on the task of regeneration. In 1789 the French General Assembly began to wipe out every symbol of the unregenerate past, 'the system of administration, the physical divisions of the country, the classes of society, the corporations, the weights and measures, the calendar'. Lastly, in its extreme, millenialist form revolution aspired to escape out of history altogether to inaugurate a new timeless order. Because the past was imperfect Turgot sought to escape entirely from its narrow confines; similarly the United States from its earliest origins: 'All through America meant: escape from History. They started fresh, unencumbered with political Past.'[27]

But in truth revolution destroyed only whig history which depended upon consensus and continuity. The historian of revolution was not a passive recorder. Rather he was a collaborator in revolution with the revolutionary. The historian became a participating revolutionary himself. 'If the Past has been an obstacle and a burden, knowledge of the Past is the safest and surest emancipation.' He clarified this complicity in his analysis of French revolutionary historiography which formed an appendix to his lectures on this subject. Referring to Michelet he wrote, 'History is resurrection. The historian is called to revise trials and reverse sentences, as the people, who are the subject of all history, awoke to the knowledge of their wrongs and of their power, and rose up to avenge the past. History is also restitution. Authorities tyrannized and nations suffered; but the Revolution is the advent of justice, and the central fact in the experience of mankind.'[28]

Acton's obsession with revolution is seen at its sharpest – and most unbalanced – in his review of James Bryce's *American Commonwealth* of 1889. Impeccable Liberal though he was, Bryce had imbibed all the conservative assumptions of the historical method from E.A.Freeman, his Oxford teacher, and his reputation had been made by his *Holy Roman Empire* of 1864 which exemplified that school's emphasis on institutional and racial continuity. Similarly, he interpreted the American Revolution as an unspectacular and limited extension of specific, traditional British liberties to the colonies. The constitution of 1787 was imbued with 'an English spirit, and therefore a conservative spirit... No men were less revolutionary in spirit than the heroes of the American Revolution.

They made a revolution in the name of Magna Charta and the Bill of Rights.' To which Acton responds, 'I descry a bewildered Whig emerging from the third volume with a reverent appreciation of ancestral wisdom, Burke's *Reflections*... and a growing belief in the function of ghosts to make laws for the quick.' He went on to accuse Bryce of deliberately over-emphasizing the counter-revolutionary tendencies of 1787 at the expense of the revolutionary spirit of 1776 in order to render the revolution retrospectively safe, to stress continuity over discontinuity, the conservatism of Washington, Hamilton and Marshall over the radicalism of Jefferson and Madison. Most seriously, Bryce's stress on Anglo-American institutional continuity and legal borrowings ignored the colonies' initial appeal to natural, unwritten law, 'the boundless innovation, the unfathomed gulf', to justify their independence. That appeal to abstract justice transformed the events of 1776 into a liberal act, for the 'story of the revolted colonies impresses us first and most distinctly as the supreme manifestation of the law of resistance, as the abstract revolution in its purest and most perfect shape'.[29]

Acton's explicit aim in the review was to undermine the implicit conservatism of the historical method and to balance Bryce's complacent interpretation of the United States as a little England writ large. But his own wilful distortion and emotional unbalance hint at deeper unconscious motives at work. Bryce's influential book had once more revealed the character of the historian's complicity through interpretation; his temporizing, fudging nature had imposed a false traditionalism upon American experience. 'The two American presidents who agreed in saying that Whig and Tory belong to natural history, proposed a dilemma which Mr. Bryce wishes to elude. He prefers to stand halfway between the two, and to resolve general principles into questions of expediency, probability, and degree.' This was the essence of whig history Acton determined to destroy. Politically, like Tocqueville, Bryce thought of one country while writing of another, saw 1888 in 1776, and by implication this served to extinguish the current prospects of Gladstonian revolution. Where Acton had interpreted the American example as a thorn, Bryce had offered a cushion. For Acton the United States affirmed the legitimacy of revolution for all times; it 'invites the nations to revolt on metaphysical grounds'; 'European revolutions have been just, *a fortiori*, if the American revolution was just.'[30] Personally, Bryce's history implied formidable limitations to each individual's potential for genuine innovation, and if this was true of Jefferson in 1776 – if Jefferson merely took up and extended the politics of Burke and Chatham – then it was equally true of Acton in 1889. It denied that human capacity for emancipating renewal which nourished Acton's imagination at its deepest level and offered, perhaps, an obscure form of psychological therapy which helped to dispel the burdensome fixations of a personal history.

But if Acton was right, where did the revolution terminate? Bryce had emptied America of its revolutionary content. Acton's study of the French Revolution had traced the descent into the Jacobin reign of terror with all its dogmatic inhumanity, before concluding ominously with Napoleon's firing of blank cartridges in the coup d'état of Brumaire in 1799. He refused to accept that history was nothing more than an interminable – and pointless – cyclical pattern. Instead, because providence was progress, he invested revolution with a redemptive function. If modern history was the advent of the reign of ideas, it was the task of the revolutionary and the historian to assist in the birth of the ideal state. But what was the ideal state? The answer was suspiciously totalitarian. Acton had never conceded two sides to every question: there was only one court of final appeal. Like Plato he conceived of the ideal. 'He sets his aim at the thought of God. He follows a Kingdom that exists in an ideal world.' And yet Plato was profoundly undemocratic and had expelled poets from the Republic. Be it Gregory VII or Calvin, Mazzini, William Lloyd Garrison or Bismarck, Acton had consistently opposed the imposition of abstract absolutism. Consciously he employed every mechanical device to hand – a free Church, conciliarism, federalism, a bicameral system – to break power up and disperse it. Yet unconsciously, and it is the central paradox of Acton's thinking, he still yearned for a universal state where there were not two sides to every question, nor truth relative. Privately he grasped the dire implications: 'Government by idea tends to take in everything, to make the whole of society obedient to the idea. Spaces not so governed are unconquered, beyond the border, unconverted, unconvinced, a future danger.' 'An ideal government, much better, perhaps, would have to be maintained by effort, and imposed by force.'[31] Publicly the *History of Freedom* remained unwritten, not because it was the history of that which was not (Acton never blenched at the prospect of recording the infinite varieties of original sin as they manifested themselves in time) but rather because that history would force to the surface an unresolved conflict, a chilling recognition that the revolution would issue out of violence not into the coming of Christ's kingdom on earth, but into a tyranny far more horrendous than Acton dared conceive of.

5 The Historian

Early in 1894 Gladstone resigned over the issue of naval estimates, and Lord Rosebery assumed the premiership from March until June in the following year. During his brief span of office, the last ebbing moments of nineteenth-century Liberal power, both Seeley and Froude died and the Prime Minister was faced with the problem of having to find two new Regius professors. At Oxford he appointed his old Christ Church tutor, Frederick York Powell, and to Cambridge he sent the sixty-one-year-old Lord Acton. The choice had not been an easy one. Oscar Browning, Rosebery's one-time Etonian master, had importunately thrust forward his prior claims. The names of Maitland and Prothero had been canvassed: the former was considered too young at forty-five and too legal a historian, and Sir William Harcourt thought the latter too dull. Strangely enough it was Gladstone, supported by that other great pillar of the Anglican establishment, Queen Victoria, who opposed the appointment of a Catholic to the chair. But Kimberley urged Acton's poverty and his loyalty in the Lords on political grounds, while Creighton and Bryce threw their academic weight into the balance to secure the appointment. After some rapid searching a copy of the *Sendschreiben* was found to spare Acton the embarrassment of arriving at a university whose library didn't possess a single publication by its new professor.

Initially Acton displayed little enthusiasm. He rather gathered that the History faculty was weak and that Cambridge displayed little interest in or curiosity about the subject, 'And as my predecessor did not awaken it, there is no chance of my doing much.' Yet the venture was a success for all that. He took up rooms in Nevile's Court in Trinity College, helped found the college history society (to it he read his paper on his 'Archival Tour'), encouraged undergraduate and graduate alike, lectured enthusiastically on modern European history and the French Revolution, embarked on the massive task of editing the *Cambridge Modern History*, and wisely avoided as much administration as possible. To the young G.M. Trevelyan he was an exotic specimen, a 'sage of immense and mysterious distinction, famous in old Continental controversies... a traveller from the antique lands of European statecraft, religion and learning, with the brow of Plato above the reserved and epigrammatic lips of the diplomatist'. A shy classicist at King's, E.M.Forster, attended his lectures on the French Revolution and was struck by their wisdom: 'I knew that something was passing me, and copied into a note book: "Every villain is followed by a sophist with a sponge."'[1]

If this final Cambridge period proved serene and rewarding despite the tedious grind of the *CMH*, why the early misgivings and the later surprise at enjoying the post? Mamy, his daughter, offers a clue when she writes that an academic life was considered unnatural to one of Acton's social background. Seeley and Froude, Kingsley and Freeman had all come from the clerical middle classes and finally reaped the rewards of an increasingly professional academic establishment in salaries and appointments. Acton was an aristocrat of impeccable credentials who had married a Dalberg, the first among the nobility of the Holy Roman Empire, and he tended rather to look down on grubby middle-class professionalism as a form of 'trade'. Despite an amicable working relationship with Bryce he was distressed by his 'terrible traces of middle-class nonconformity'. His own family had served the state for generations out of a high sense of *noblesse oblige* as ministers, cardinals and admirals. During the 1870s the enticing prospect of high political office beckoned with its dazzling possibility of enacting history rather than merely recording it. His scholarship was a consuming passion far beyond the mild antiquarian concerns of country clerics on whom time weighed heavily, yet it remained for all that an essentially private and amateur concern which could be dropped when the great game of politics called. When those grandiose ambitions collapsed with the passing of Gladstone there was only the salve of academic distinction – honorary degrees at Oxford and Cambridge and an honorary fellowship at All Souls, Oxford – to comfort him, but he remained determinedly unprofessional: there was never any grammar-school boy imperative to publish in order to procure tenure or land a provincial chair.

But this did not prevent him from co-operating with those professional academics who did; with Bryce, Creighton, A.W.Ward, Henry Sidgwick, Freeman, R.L.Poole and York Powell who together founded the *English Historical Review* in 1885. By insisting on the highest standards, urging more foreign contributors and less insularity, and in launching its reputation by contributing his famous article on 'The German School of History' he became, in Creighton's words, 'its prop and stay'.[2] Ten years later he embarked upon the editorship of the *CMH* – a whole choir of madonnas – which submerged him in endless tedium and worry. C.H.Firth had to be prodded into writing more, J.B.Bury's interminable essay on 'The Ottoman Conquest' ruthlessly cut, one outrageous jingo's prejudices watered down, other chapters from historians bound in buckram (the phrase is Acton's) lightened a little, various Americans – Captain Mahan, James Ford Rhodes, Woodrow Wilson – netted, and the great to-do over Henry C. Lea's critical chapter on 'The Eve of the Reformation' sorted out. So many promising commissions, such as Leslie Stephen's on Victorian intellectual life and Frederic Harrison's on early-nineteenth-century French thought, never materialized, and of the five writers who were required, in Acton's Prospectus, to keep their various religious beliefs out of their chapters so that no reader would know when one put down his pen and another took it up, only one, Fairburn, a Congregationalist, eventually contributed. Promises from the other four – Gasquet (Catholic), Liebermann (Hebrew), Stubbs

(Anglican) and Harrison (Positivist) – evaporated. The onerous project diverted him from his own work, frittered away precious hours and finally broke him, much as the *Dictionary of National Biography* broke Leslie Stephen. In 1901 he resigned both chair and editorship following a stroke and he died the following year at Tegernsee. The *CMH* fell into the duller hands of Ward, Stanley Leathes and G.W.Prothero, and Acton was alike condemned for insisting upon an unobtainable definitive history and blamed for the conventional chapters that emerged.

To understand Acton's philosophy of history it is essential to appreciate his interpretation of the nineteenth-century revolution in historical method of which he was in many ways the apogee. He dated its origins from the French Revolution and the Napoleonic wars which swept disconcertingly through Europe and intruded into the sedentary lives of German professors who had grown accustomed to keeping history safely bound in dusty folios. Like the legitimist statesmen at Vienna, they wished to tame this brutal interruption, return the genie to its lamp, and join together the links snapped by revolution. But despite their wish to return to the securities of the pre-1789 world, they had first to destroy the Enlightenment writings of Diderot, Jefferson and Hume and the desiccating rationalism of Newton and Voltaire which had led to such a perilous *dénouement* at the end of the century. It was the desire to destroy those eighteenth-century phantoms of the infallible conscience, the universal and unwritten law, the *a priori* principles of eternal justice, which led the German historical school to inaugurate an intellectual revolution as profound as that of the Renaissance rediscovery of the classical world, and rekindle the lost vision of medieval Christianity. The eighteenth century had extended the realm of reason but at the expense of destroying revelation and had ended the persecution of witches only by the casting out of devils and the destruction of a sense of sin. It was the wish to reaffirm 'the divine fire at the centre' – so markedly absent from the historical writings of Gibbon, Robertson and Hume

– which led the new school to reject the metaphysics of natural law and replace a mechanistic, Newtonian view of society by an organic one which would reach back to the healing spring of the Middle Ages. The medieval revival became a pilgrimage, 'a return to continuity in social institutions, to tradition in ideas, and to history in science', and with its profoundly conservative implications it nurtured a new respect for the past, for patriotic sentiments and ancient hereditary privileges. This nineteenth-century renaissance was accomplished with the aid of the Romantic school, itself 'the revolt of outraged history', which demanded an imaginative recreation of the past, a recognition that it was something other than the present, and which contributed to a general heightening of historical consciousness and the sense of each individual as the product of historical forces. 'Truth,' Newman wrote, 'is the daughter of time. In a higher world it is otherwise, but here below to live is to change, and to be perfect is to have changed often.'[3]

But Newman's theology was only one of a multiplicity of disciplines which absorbed the new historical spirit; Savigny and Maine were to employ it in jurisprudence, Strauss and Feuerbach in their biblical studies, Comte in his philosophy. Once a servant, history now became master; no longer just one branch of knowledge, it became the mode and method employed in each and every discipline, and as it did so the eighteenth-century absolute order dissolved; abstract systems were resolved into processes, deductive principles were toppled and subjected to inductive reassessment, the definitive yielded to the relative, the change was away from 'the solid conclusion to the process which led up to it, from the discovered law to the law of discovery'.[4]

Thus a method initially intended to restore ended by imposing a disruptive and uncertain historical relativism. It endowed the historian with immense prestige and made him master of each discipline. He could create or destroy, rehabilitate or undermine, but what he could no longer do was assert and confirm a universal moral order. Instead numberless 'systems and opinions lose their absolute character, and appear in their conditional relative truth when the mode of their formation and the modifying influences of time and place are understood'. Any number of attempts were made to escape this relativistic prison. If history was change then inexorable laws governing that change must be discernible, a positivistic system must be discovered to determine the pattern of historical destiny and prophesy mankind's inevitable future. The concoction of historical laws captured much of the declining faith in religion and harnessed the ascending belief in the sciences, and writers like Buckle, Hegel, Marx and Gobineau identified heredity, race, the *Weltgeist*, climate, evolution, class, survival or whatever as the determining principle. 'Science was propitiated with visions of unity and continuity; religion, by the assurance of incessant progress; politics, by the ratification of the past,' and in each case 'the confused conflict of free wills' succumbed to 'the simplicity of resistless cause'. The majority of humbler historians spurned such all-encompassing explanations, yet they too, locked within time, could offer no certitude, only a distorting light shone on the past from the present. 'As each age,' Acton wrote, 'so is its view of the Past.'[5]

Acton was profoundly aware that a history which merely reflected the present was the very essence of whiggism, and yet Herbert Butterfield has accused him of being an arch-whig. Not only is this not so, it is possible to go further and assert categorically that Acton's entire historical canon is nothing less than a sustained assault on every variety of whig present-mindedness. And really it is not surprising that Acton should have been so alive to this fallacy, for just as his early struggles had centred on the ultramontane's sanctification of the present spiritual order, so his later attacks concentrated politically on apologists like Maine who sought good reasons for adopted policy. All whig historians were by extension ultras, for, however various the causes they defended, their ultimate purpose was to apotheosize the present dispensation. The whig cause was progress but progress of a peculiarly circumscribed sort, finding its consummation seemingly in Macaulay and the principles of the first Reform Bill. And because Macaulay relentlessly distorted to confirm and ratify the settled, current order, he denied history's separate autonomy and worth, and devalued it to the extent that his writings constituted 'a key to half the prejudices of our age'. Acton grasped the implications of this bias as early as 1858 in a review of R.K.Philp's *History of Progress in Great Britain*.

> It is in reality the notion of perpetual progress which lies at the bottom of this style of historical writing. It comes from admiration of the present, not the past. The writer who brought it into vogue was Macaulay... The partisans of the theory of indefinite progress forfeit all the advantage which is to be got from the contemplation of those points on which former ages were superior to our own... We are unable and care not, to understand and sympathize with them. The true view of history is the reverse of this narrowness... Each event and period of history must be viewed in its own native light. It is the business of historians everywhere to furnish us with this light, without which each object is distorted and discoloured.

Macaulay imposed a preconceived framework which made for a cramped vision and an 'unsuggestive fixity'. 'He never starts except for the end in view. His hook and bait will only catch a particular fish, – there is no vague cast of the net.'[6]

What his net caught was success, achievement, history's winners. When a writer separated experience from morality, pragmatic observation compelled him to use the sole criterion of results by which to measure what was 'right'. Providence was justified by the event; those forces to be reckoned with were those forces which prevailed; power went where power was due and 'the conquering cause was the favourite of the gods'. Implicit in this ethic of the *fait accompli* was a determinism which confirmed the goddess Necessity and fixed fates, a history which celebrated the inevitable victor. The reverse side of this coin was the neglect of failure and an indifference to the paths not taken. The whig had little to say on Louis XVI or the Jacobites, and yet Acton believed that there was 'much more to say, than anyone now supposes, for many a lost cause', and such forgotten topics as sorcery, the deposing power, the Ptolemaic system and sea serpents.[7] Whig history was a history devoid of contingency; armed with hindsight it ignored the infinite number of possibilities available at each juncture; knowing the outcome in advance it drained the narrative of its complex openness.

Obsessed by the politics of achieved power whig writers were fatally addicted to hero-worship and to the Promethean superman whose strident will was above the law. Carlyle, Morley, Froude, Firth and Gardiner hovered like moths round the flame of the powerful historical force embodied in a Cromwell or a Frederick the Great. Physical dominion, brute strength and military conquest led Charles Kingsley to write of Attila the Hun and Tamburlaine the Great. Louis XIV was held up in textbooks as a model for schoolchildren to admire while his six million subjects who starved on grass went unmentioned. Acton vigorously questioned the assumption that conquest and enslavement indicated inherent superiority, but the whig school continued to remain dazzled by power and to serve as its obedient accomplice. In the lecture theatre E.M.Forster had written down an abbreviated version of Acton's dictum: 'The strong man with the dagger is followed by the weaker man with the sponge. First, the criminal who slays; then the sophist who defends the slayer.'[8]

The whig required a cause to fight for and an ineluctable law to advance. Devoid of disinterestedness, he was compelled to serve and sacrifice his precious independence. Thus Droysen glorified Prussian militarism, Macaulay the Whig Party, Thiers the Bonapartists, and all of them pre-eminently the manifest destiny of nationalism. In England the common national assumption of innate superiority took the historical form of a preordained advance towards ordered self-government and pragmatic liberties which were both envied and misapplied elsewhere. English history, so the whigs would have their readers believe, was the unexampled annals of a tolerant, peace-loving society which spontaneously rose up to defeat the alien despotism of the Stuart dynasty and secure the sublime freedoms of a bloodless revolution. Acton would have none of this. England progressed through sanguinary reigns, flourished under the harsher regime of the Tudors and alighted upon its constitution through a combination of luck, fraud and treason. If England endured it was not because of the independent, magnanimous spirit of her people, but rather despite their 'consistent, uninventive, stupid fidelity'. Where else would a Prime Minister like the Earl of Liverpool, endowed with 'a mind impervious to thought', have survived through fifteen tumultuous years? Liberty was never the supreme desire of the English heart. Cromwell was an enemy of all free institutions. Locke, the patron saint of the whigs, however reasonable and sensible, was a typical trimmer, the theoretician of an order which ensured the dominion of property, hierarchy and the divine right of landowners. The Bill of Rights, apotheosized by the whigs, was dismissed as 'narrow, spiritless, confused, tame, and unsatisfactory', a characteristically niggardly assertion of freedoms.[9]

Macaulay's *History* was shaped by a belief in evolution, consensus, moderation and the easy optimism born of a belief in inevitable progress. It pivoted on the bloodless revolution of 1688 but only at the expense of the subversive writings of Lilburne and Harrington who grappled with deeper issues of conscience and soul in the years of civil disorder which preceded it. Acton read deeply in the republican outpourings of the seventeenth century and encouraged G.P.Gooch to explore this neglected terrain further. Because the whig was obliged to tell a tale which had an uplifting moral and a happy ending, a chronicle of temporary setbacks but ultimate triumphs, he consistently underplayed every darker aspect and bleaker undercurrent.

Whig history took the form of celebration partly because it was preoccupied with tangibles rather than the unyielding mysteries of the soul, and it was easier to be optimistic about the former than the latter. Macaulay admired 1688 because it ushered in an age of economic supremacy, imperial expansion and an ethos dedicated to the confirmation of oligarchic privilege which secured the world of the Holland House set which he so much admired. His famous third chapter on the social and economic life of the nation gloried in the externals of profit and trade, the growth of cities and accumulation of wealth, the pure physics of Newton and the practical technological innovations of Watt and Arkwright. These to him were proofs of progress, steeped as he was in the nineteenth-century worship of material advance. It was a history as retailed by Gradgrind, of facts without vision and narrative without revelation. Devoid of a spiritual or ethical dimension, he succeeded in moving history out of the sacristy only to place it at the disposal of the parliamentary lobby. This was the outward 'progress' that Newman dismissed as a slang term and Acton as the religion of those who had none. Even Macaulay's understanding of liberty was materialistic, based as it was on the protection and preservation of property, the cautious extension of the franchise to those who had a tangible stake in society, and a future vision pitched at no higher level of spirituality than that each Englishman be allowed his immemorial right to roast beef and a pint of ale. The only advantage of his bland, self-congratulatory patriotism lay in its relative harmlessness when placed beside his German nationalist counterparts. There Sybel, Mommsen, Gneist, Bernhardi, Drucker, Droysen and Treitschke glorified a far more ominous military tradition and held Berlin like a fortress.

Macaulay was the most successful of a popular school. He wrote graphically, was easy to read, had a good plot, left no problem unsolved and confirmed each reader's prejudice. But other historians were also tempted to fail in their high calling, elide difficulties, simplify complexities and evade the full rigours of truth-telling. Mandell Creighton for one preferred 'the larger public that takes history in the shape of literature, to scholars whose souls are vexed with the insolubility of problems and who get their meals in the kitchen'. Ranke was another: his history was 'all plums and no suet. It is all garnish, but no beef... He is an epicure and likes only tit-bits.'[10] But these two historians had a graver charge to answer, for while Ranke 'enjoyed the luxury of indecision', Creighton passed over history 'with a serene curiosity, a suspended judgment, a divided jury, and a pair of white gloves'. Acton pitted himself against whiggism pre-eminently because it made predetermined forces and not individuals the arbiters of history. Because men obeyed the spirit of the age rather than moulded it, whiggism assigned little choice to the individual, and with the absence of choice went moral responsibility and blame. Inasmuch as each individual conformed to and confirmed the *Zeitgeist* it excused and exonerated crimes. With Buckle the individual was absorbed entirely in the wake of statistical averages, yet Acton passionately believed that with the disappearance of choice went the possibility of freedom. Since his early reversal he understood the Inquisition to be the instrument of personal decisions, taken separately by Ximenes, Torquemada, Peter Arbues, Sixtus IV. Each could have helped dismantle that hideous machinery; each chose not to. History was full of victims and suffering and yet whig history provided no criminals. In the gradual growth of things individuals either contributed to the present order and were deemed 'good', or they did not, in which case they were 'bad' or vanished altogether. Acton's indictment of whig errors was unfair to Macaulay, and unfairer still to Locke: it was as severe as it was comprehensive. Like ultramontanism its ultimate purpose was not to question or indict but to canonize and confirm, and in so doing to 'perpetuate the reign of sin and acknowledge the sovereignty of wrong', when it was 'the part of real greatness to know how to stand and fall alone, stemming, for a lifetime, the contemporary flood'.[11]

But how did Acton intend to stem the contemporary flood and escape the pitfalls which vitiated whig history? What did he propose to offer in its stead? History possessed the one inestimable advantage of dealing with incontrovertible facts, and the historian's task was to collect the evidence and scientifically reconstruct a certain sequence of events that occurred in time. That the earth revolved round the sun, that the Donation of Constantine was a palpable forgery, were of the same order of data, equally capable of being tested and verified. History was the one unassailable revelation of God's dealing with man, and truth in history resolved itself into matters of fact. Acton never underestimated the task; it was immense because the materials were inexhaustible. The past was intractable, slow to yield up its secrets, but though the process of reconstruction was infinitely difficult it was not strictly impossible. It required enormous stamina. To fudge the onerous duty of archival work, to base premature verdicts on a paucity of materials as Carlyle had done when a sneeze from a fellow researcher sent him fleeing from the British Museum reading room, was to shirk duty. An exacting and discriminating art was required, insight and imagination, to draw evidence from often unpropitious, stony material. Each document had to be scrutinized to assess its veracity and worth. What was the writer's motive? Was he telling the truth? What did a letter's recipient expect? The evidence might be an exercise in subterfuge and duplicity, deliberately intended to mislead or betray, or even an unconscious exercise in self-delusion. Secondary materials added to the complexity and the whole process of rigorous examination had to be repeated and extended. History had to include the history of histories, and the letters of historians had to be scrutinized as carefully as primary documents. The historian himself was on trial, treated as suspect and witness, his motives and veracity investigated. Reconstruction required both knowing and unknowing, a deliberate curtailing of hindsight along with a fuller appreciation of those unrecognized forces propelling events forward which the actors were, at the time, unaware of. 'Our business is to know what contemporaries could not tell us because they could not see it.' The opening of private archives exposed the 'unpremeditated self-revelation of correspondence' and enabled the historian to probe behind the façade of official documents to the nebulous realm of interior motivation. For too long historians like Ranke had relied on state papers and consequently provided an official version of events. Acton sought for a science of character, a historical psychology which would reveal the inside as well as the outside of things, expose 'the inner point of view, the *raison d'être*'. In this he was assisted by the writings of George Eliot. Like her, the historian must contrive to creep inside the skin of his participants, see the world through their eyes, before recovering his independence, standing back and 'stripping off the borrowed shell, and exposing scientifically and indifferently the soul of a Vestal, a Crusader, an Anabaptist, an Inquisitor, a Dervish, a Nihilist, or a Cavalier without attraction, preference, or caricature'.[12] Impartiality was obligatory, a dispassionate love of truth for its own sake, what Michelet called *le désintéressement des morts*. Acton wrote to Simpson in 1859 that 'our studies ought to be all but purposeless. They want to be pursued with chastity, like mathematics.' Thirty-nine years later in his Prospectus for the *CMH* he repeated the advice to a younger generation of historians: 'We shall avoid the needless utterance of opinion, and the service of a cause... Contributors will understand that we are established, not under the Meridian of Greenwich, but in Long. 30° w; that our Waterloo must be one that satisfies French and English, Germans and Dutch alike.' Detachment was all the more imperative because the historian worked on partial and biased sources.

It is melancholy to think what would become of our knowledge of the past, but for the passions, interests, and prejudices which are the means of preserving the history they distort. The annals of happy nations are vacant; and annalists if they were wiser would probably be less industrious. It requires an impartial man to make a good historian; but it is the partial and onesided who hunt out the materials. If all writers were disinterested and sincere, history would not be filled with lies. But there is falsehood enough to keep up the investigation of truth, and plenty of men, patient, laborious, and passionate, to provide materials.[13]

So far so good and, as far as it goes, unexceptional enough. But Acton went one step further to clinch his anti-whig counter-strategy by means of moral judgement. He had not always believed that the historian should judge and Döllinger had urged the superfluity of moral standards. 'We are no wiser when we know that one is good or bad... It is the business of Him to judge who can carry His judgements into effect.'[14] Now, imbued with an immense optimism about scientific history, Acton believed that complete understanding allowed for confident judgement. If history dealt with hanging matters nobody should be hanged on damaged testimony, but if the accumulated evidence was unequivocal and damning, sentence could be appropriately passed. Turning Mme de Staël's famous dictum — 'Tout comprendre, c'est tout pardonner' — on its head, he held that 'To understand all was to judge all.' But why the desire to judge at all once the evidence had been presented? The conundrum posed in the first chapter, the apparent discrepancy between scientific history and unscientific judgements, is resolved, for Acton held that it was judgement that made history scientific; it constituted the final stage of reconstruction, a recognition of having attained a position of complete understanding and absolute impartiality, of imprinting history with the definitive stamp of scientific credentials. His solution to the practical problem of present-mindedness, of the historian being in time and serving its cause, was to escape out of time altogether by bringing a timeless moral absolute to bear. That moral absolute was the ethical teaching of the New Testament which was immutable and after which 'Everything new is old.' The aim was 'to fix the anchor of one's ethics in something apart from liquid opinion', to rescue history from the contemporary and transient, so that it became 'our deliverer not only from the undue influence of other times, but from the undue influence of our own, from the tyranny of environment, and the pressure of the air we breathe'. As Gertrude Himmelfarb rightly observes, Acton imposes judgement on history rather than deriving judgement from it, and confronts apologetic with conscientious history. Again and again he juxtaposes 'science' and 'judgement' as if they were synonymous: 'Conscience cannot prevail in politics without science'; 'it is the office of historical science to maintain morality as the sole impartial criterion of men and things'; he sentenced to hanging 'for reasons of quite obvious justice; still more, still higher, for the sake of historical science'.[15]

Acton could apply an ideal, external standard because, however feeble its flame in the records of profane history, its presence was very real to him. 'We contemplate our ideas in the sunlight of heaven, and apply them in the darkness of earth.' 'Opinions alter, manners change, creeds rise and fall, but the moral law is written on the tablets of eternity.'[16] Again, judgement answered to the historian's compelling need to impose some ordering principle, a coherent pattern on the chaos of disparate, unconnected facts which crowd in upon him, and helped him to distinguish the significant from the irrelevant. Acton was an obsessive list-maker; of famous bachelors, of pre-Reformation reformers, of ministers who were also cardinals. Eleven thousand and sixteen lines were numbered in a notebook in preparation for a vast scheme of historical literature. Without an overarching vision history was emptied of any meaning and became instead a pointless Sisyphean ebb and flow. Most vitally, the reinstatement of conscience returned history to individuals and deprived the whigs of their trick of evoking God in the cause of princes.

But this attempt to transform justice into science masked more emotional promptings, the greatest of which was the itch to punish. The Gospels spread Christ's message of love and humility: 'Blessed are the meek: for they shall inherit the earth. Blessed are the pure in heart: for they shall see God.' And yet, despite his atonement for the world's sins, Christ's kingdom on earth had not come to pass. Acton's advice for those wishing to write history was, 'Don't,' for to do so was to enter one by one into the circles of Dante's Inferno. Sin flourished, power dominated, the virtuous must expect to suffer wrongs; the path by which men passed to freedom was 'dreary and heart-breaking', and at times Acton wished only that the long agony might cease.[17] With the tools of scientific method historians could now tear down the outward seeming and uncover a dark interior world which revealed far more conscious sin than unconscious error. 'Use of history,' he wrote, 'no surprises. He has seen all this before. He knows what constant and invariable forces will resist the truth and the Higher Purpose. What weakness, division, excess, will damage the better cause. The splendid plausibility of error, the dazzling attractiveness of sin. And by what adjustment to inferior motives good causes succeed.' Once more he was influenced by the novels of George Eliot, that 'consummate expert in the pathology of conscience'.[18] Having first laid bare her characters' motives she then exacted an earthly retribution from them, holding that wrongs could not be committed without consequent suffering. Nemesis stalks through her works as in a Sophoclean drama: in *Middlemarch* Bulstrode's long-kept scandalous secret is finally exposed; Dorothea Brooke suffers but is enlightened by her suffering. But George Eliot had authorial licence. Having created her imaginary characters she could control them, enter the novel to draw a moral and conclude by applying salutary justice. Historical figures were neither created nor invented; they existed in a real world and lived a life quite independent of the writer's control, and the moral extracted from their lives was altogether different: 'History provides neither compensation for suffering nor penalties for wrong.' Not history – but what of the historian? What if he went beyond bearing witness and, in full possession of the evidence, stepped forward to exact retributive justice?

The worst will be known, and then sentence need not be deferred. With the fulness of knowledge the pleader's occupation is gone, and the apologist is deprived of his bread.

Mendacity depended on concealment of evidence. When that is at an end, fable departs with it, and the margin of legitimate divergence is narrowed.

The historian, Christ-like, would atone for the reign of sin, and right the wrongs of the world. Thus Acton's plea to his Cambridge audience, 'suffer no man and no cause to escape the undying penalty which history has the power to inflict on wrong.' And to Creighton, 'Historic responsibility has to make up for the want of legal responsibility.'[19]

It was to Creighton, author of *A History of the Papacy During the Reformation*, that Acton fully developed his theory of judgement. The correspondence is a famous set-piece and it is generally assumed that the two were poles apart and that Creighton, who disapproved of judgement in history, won because he was right. In fact there was considerable agreement and concession on both sides. The initial point at issue was not whether Sixtus IV was to be condemned for implementing the Inquisition, which Acton admitted depended on one's point of view, but whether Sixtus was personally responsible for its continuation, which was a question of historical fact, and on this Creighton capitulated, having admitted obfuscating the question of papal responsibility. Even the famous dictum thrown up by the correspondence was uncharacteristically qualified. 'Power *tends* to corrupt and *absolute* power corrupts absolutely. Great men are *almost always* bad men.' To prove this Acton appealed to a simple moral code with murder as a 'scientific zero', but Creighton responded by suggesting that this standard was hopelessly simplified, that there must be a more flexible sliding scale with subtler degrees of criminality. How, for example, would Acton apply his 'scientific zero' in the case of a careless doctor called in to minister to a dying patient? Creighton was on strong ground here because Acton's 'common code' was disingenuous and contradicted by his own highly developed sense of history's complexity. Acton had himself argued that accomplice and apologist were more culpable than the criminal. Homicide could be committed by calumny as well as by dose and dagger, and legally by war. Acton appealed to a commonplace morality but could hardly expect to gain general consent for applying the hangman's noose to the neck of the benign Creighton himself for palliating Sixtus' record, and with the collapse of his universally acceptable code went his science of judgement. Creighton pressed home his advantage. To clarify his case Acton had emphasized palpable crimes over uncertain motives, but Creighton countered by pointing out that criminal laws also changed to reflect changed moral attitudes; heresy was no longer a crime and men were no longer hanged for sheep-stealing as they were in the eighteenth century. If Sixtus ordered the burning of heretics it was because Christian opinion regarded heresy as a supreme threat. 'Society is an organism and its laws are an expression of the conditions which it considers necessary for its own preservation.' However, in depicting the medieval popes as 'men like ourselves, sorely tempted by the possession of power, trammelled by holding a representative position' he conceded an unvarying consistency in human nature favourable to Acton's scientific history. Acton had conceded the plea of chronology in regard to external laws and opinion, but denied any change in interior morality; an individual's knowledge of right and wrong was immutable. The same ultramontane spirit, now limited to varieties of spiritual despotism, would have happily massacred Huguenots in sixteenth-century France; the gentle Newman, given the opportunities of Reformation Europe, would have persecuted with the zeal of Conrad of Marburg. But in maintaining an unchanging human nature Acton trapped himself into a historical position which was essentially whig. Because he underplayed those impersonal forces which shaped and moulded each individual in an infinite variety of ways, Acton himself lapsed into anachronism, worrying over why the Bill of Rights was silent on such vital matters as national education, poor laws and free trade. It was a history which was at a loss to explain why, if Newman could have persecuted in the intolerant sixteenth century, he could not also, at the same time, raise his glass in an after-dinner toast to conscience before the Pope as the nineteenth-century Newman had done.

The central point of disagreement was over Acton's refusal to excuse on grounds of rank and power, for the sanctification of office was the cardinal heresy of ultramontane and whig alike. Creighton argued that rulers were required to stoop to immoral means; as representatives and exponents of vast social forces, they were subject to intense pressures, compelled, as protectors and trustees, to put the interests and safety of their nation or Church above all else, forced to do that which was possible and expedient in a relentless struggle for survival, rather than that which was right. It was foolish for the irresponsible historian, free from such urgent pressures, to indulge in the luxury of snubbing and sneezing at those in authority from 'a pinnacle of conscious rectitude'. He found it easier to condone Sixtus IV's public support for the Spanish Inquisition than to excuse his involvement in the private vendetta of the Pazzi conspiracy against the Medici in 1478. Acton held, on the contrary, that the greater the power the greater the moral responsibility, not less. He did not concern himself with private morality, with adultery, or with Pope Alexander VI's nightly entertainment of courtesans. He wished to strip away all such irrelevancies – the fact that St Just was a thief or St Charles Borromeo a devout man – and judge by the lowest watermark of public action. He insisted on a public morality which precluded the use of immoral means to achieve ends however desirable, and opposed a M'Naghten rule which excused the abuse of arbitrary power on grounds of diminished responsibility. Murder was murder, and he recognized no distinction between Ravaillac, Henry IV's assassin, and Pius V who plotted the murder of Elizabeth I, Elizabeth who was implicated in the death of Mary Queen of Scots, or Mary herself who was probably complicit with Bothwell in the murder of her own husband Darnley. Why should Frederick the Great be excused his unprovoked attack on Silesia in 1740, while a criminal who poisoned his neighbour to obtain his property would be condemned? But here Acton was once more contradicting himself. Having previously conceded separate and distinct public and private moralities, a dual ethical system which recognized Caesar's claims as well as God's, he now blurred the distinction in a utopian insistence that Caesar yield all his temporal claims to God. Ironically the Anglican ended by lecturing the Catholic on the doctrine of original sin.

Creighton was surprised by the vehemence of Acton's response; it was, he wrote to Poole, 'ill-natured, passionate and almost incoherent', yet Acton stumbled in further. Surely judgement was superfluous, insisted Creighton. Why not simply state the case as clearly as possible and leave the reader to draw his own conclusions if he wished? This seemed sensible enough, but to Acton it both undermined his ostensible rationale for history's scientific status and, even more unforgivably, exposed the irrational compulsion to punish which underlay that doctrine.

Creighton's final thrust was to suggest that Acton's 'Architectonic' history was unwritable because it burdened the historian with an omniscience he was incapable of assuming. Since inheriting the vast collection of an Oxford predecessor who had planned an unwritten history on the rise of universities, Creighton had had a horror of non-productivity. 'I thought that I had best frankly do what I could; anything would serve as a step for my successors. So I wrote.'[20] Acton conspicuously did not. That infallibility which he denied to the Pope he readily conferred on the historian. History would reign instead of serve, and not for nothing was the CMH referred to as Acton's 'Encyclical'. There is no need to search for deeper explanations for Acton's later sterility. The more he tried, by superhuman efforts, to master his material, the greater the gap between aim and achievement yawned, a gap he attempted to narrow by yet further paralysing research. He became a prodigy of learning, but his reading stultified and inhibited his writing so that by the end he knew too much to write. His inaugural lecture on 'The Study of History' is weighed down with 105 footnotes, referring to over 300 sources, the longest alone quoting thirty-two separate authorities. They display an extraordinarily wide and impressive range of reading, but how tedious and unnecessary they are beside the lucid economy of the text! He absorbed mountains of documentation for his lectures on the French Revolution, tracing all his secondary references back to their original published sources, reading prodigious numbers of acts, *cahiers* and municipal records. For his lecture on 'The Flight to Varennes' alone he accumulated 350 record cards and consulted fifty-one separate sources.

He was over-scrupulous about writing; studying history was better, for to engage the reader's attention intricate details had to be sacrificed for effect; each sentence was a compromise, an approximation of the truth encompassed by means of a crude generalization. A blank sheet brought home to him the impossible task he had assigned to himself, and perhaps lecturing helped overcome this sensitivity which caused writer's block. He would not work with imperfect materials, knowing full well that the materials were always imperfect. And how could any document pierce to the heart of the matter, the *raison d'être*? How could the historian ever know if Caesar loved his wife, or Acton his? And yet, while scrupulously undermining the possibility, he continued to insist that Actonian history could be written. He was infinitely more successful in deploying his destructive, forensic powers against those who failed to reach his exacting standards than in writing a history which met them. Historiography was his particular forte: his 'German Schools of History', 'Döllinger's Historical Works', his study of 'The Literature of the French Revolution', and his inaugural are the four most brilliant things he wrote. He could grasp each historian's interpretation, his background, his biases and presuppositions; each ulterior motive is probed, every distortion dissected. 'I desire,' he informed his Cambridge audience, 'to rescue you from the writers of each particular school and each particular age.' Thiers writes to subvert democracy, Lamartine to exalt it, Taine to deny

free will, Louis Blanc to promote socialism; Niebuhr, projecting more current concerns into a historical void, converts the
obscure Manlius into Mirabeau, and Dean Stanley puts Lord
Shaftesbury into the Reformation. Each historian, he believed,
had to be relentlessly cross-examined as witness, and yet
Acton exempted himself from this useful exercise. Showered
with so many gifts, one of the most essential of all to a historian, that of self-knowledge, was denied him.

Like many a privileged and precocious child, Acton had
delighted in shocking nanny, and because nanny did not scold
but indulged him, teasing became a life-long habit of the
Wunderkind. In this sense Herbert Butterfield's criticism of
Acton's hubris, his proposals for a presumptuous omniscience in
historical writing, was salutary and overdue. Yet at the same
time no one did more than Butterfield to contribute to and
compound our current misunderstanding of Acton. His *Whig
Interpretation of History* (1931) had argued that Acton was
whig because he judged. Having written his own lushly whig-
gish *Englishman and His History* (1944) as his contribution
to the war effort, he returned to Acton in 1961 in a festschrift
for Dr Gooch where he reversed his earlier opinion and now
portrayed Acton as a predominantly Catholic historian possessed of an 'amazing intellectual integrity'. Yet this reversal
failed to link Acton's Catholicism with his anti-whiggism or
to recognize that his ethical history was aimed precisely at
establishing that 'self-emptying' which Butterfield demanded
of historians. Between these two radically divergent interpre-
tations he published his *History and Human Relations* (1951)
in which he retreated from his position of 1931 by suggesting,
not that judgement was inherently wrong, but that the historian never knew enough to judge; that is, his objections were
now technical not theoretical. Now, finding himself uncom-
fortably close, he falsely accused Acton of excessive severity,
and of judging without full knowledge. Butterfield's confu-
sions and contradictions, his obsessive revisions and reversals,
stemmed from his sharing a common Christian concern with
providence, and from the fact that Acton reflected and magni-

fied rather than resolved the problems for both theologian and historian. Both believed in a history endowed by God with meaning, in providence not chance, while confessing that the divine pattern was fairly inscrutable. Butterfield dispensed with this problem by severely narrowing the range of the technical historian, while Acton evaded it by projecting Christ's imminent coming into an indefinite future. Butterfield placed excessive emphasis on Acton's judgemental history because he had scoured the record cards where Acton worried such matters to death, and tended to ignore the published writings where such imponderables were peripheral to the task of narrating. The real disagreement was not over judgement so much as whether moral values should be carried into history, but here too Butterfield was inconsistent. For while advocating a strict moral neutrality, he held, simultaneously, that Acton was entirely correct in protesting against contemporary slackness in historical judgement and 'rightly indignant' about the casual handling of important moral questions.[21]

The authority accorded to Butterfield's misunderstandings is curious, for even a cursory reading of Acton would help to dispel many persistent myths surrounding him. The most stubborn is that he wrote nothing when in fact he wrote a good deal. This particular myth grew mainly because the *History of Freedom* remained unwritten, but partly, too, because what he did write was rarely 'straight' history but an unclassifiable combination of history, political theory and historiography which satisfied nobody, much of which appeared in obscure journals uncollected to this day. There was a substantial journalistic outpouring in the 1860s and by the age of forty he had written over 400 articles and reviews. Thereafter the stream became a trickle, though he wrote another fifty-eight articles in all and, in total, over eighty large-scale essays or lectures. If this is a crude, quantitative measure of achievement it answers the equally crude quantitative charge of his critics. Yet this tediously repeated accusation contains an implicit qualitative evaluation in suggesting disappointment at unfulfilled promise and unrealized potential;

few historians have worried over the fact that Acton's Oxford counterpart, Frederick York Powell, wrote not a single book on his own.

Another common assumption is that Acton wore a black cap and entered history with a Malthusian desire to depopulate it, when in reality he was very sparing in his judgements. In his lectures on modern history he publicly disavowed his St Bartholomew Massacre conspiracy theory of 1869, refused to bring in a verdict of guilty on Mary Queen of Scots' complicity in her husband's murder because of lack of evidence, and went to great lengths to be fair to those instruments of the Counter-Reformation – the Roman Inquisition, the Index and the Jesuit order – where he could be expected to be severe; 'We cannot,' he wrote, 'take our history out of Newgate.' Having cautioned his audience on the question of exculpating political crimes he proposed to avoid 'the spectacles that degrade, and the plaintive severity that agitates and wearies' in his lectures on the French Revolution. He did not keep this promise, however, because the reign of terror carried him into a chamber of horrors and the company of malefactors. Yet he held Jacobin republican principles to be at least as respectable as the *émigrés*' monarchical doctrines, and though Robespierre had evoked divine sanction for his ruthless political ends, making him 'the most hateful character in the forefront of history since Machiavelli reduced to a code the wickedness of public men', he brought about the most radical change ever in French society at the cost of a few thousand lives, far fewer than any battle in Napoleon's military campaigns fought 'for no worthier motive than ambition'.[22]

If Acton's history was providential it took the form of a vague teleology and not a restricted predetermined structure in which God rumbles audibly from the wings. The historian tends to take God's place, but the deified historian is at best semi-omniscient, observer not creator, Greek chorus rather than supreme judge. Possessing a choric foreknowledge of what is to come, having a more distinct sense of the interplay of forces denied to the participants in the drama itself, Acton simply acknowledged the historian's inescapably privileged position. This extra-perception allowed him to range backwards and forwards through time, alive to a mysterious unfolding destiny, which is given greater tragic significance by the literary device of anticipatory prolepsis. The approach of the starving women of Paris forces Marie Antoinette to flee from the Trianon which she will never see again: on the evening of 30 June 1791, Louis XVI and his brother, the Count of Provence, dine together for the last time: 'That night their ways parted, leading the one to the guillotine, and the other to the throne which had been raised by Napoleon above every throne on earth.' This privileged insight heightens rather than precludes compassion. Louis' execution is not inevitable nor is he a pawn moved across the board at the historian's whim. He is shown vainly attempting to stem the revolutionary tide, tossed to and fro by a foolish, vindictive wife, divided counsels, errors of judgement and weakness of character, and is almost invariably the author of his fate. 'There is another word for the expiation of guilt; but the wages of folly are payable here below.'[23]

Acton's faith in progress rested in its inevitable future, aware that its advance in the past had been tardy and irregular. Progress had met with intense conflict, emerged through convulsions and catastrophes, and always the balance remained uncertain as it developed along diagonals. He knew full well that error was as potent as truth, that good could come from evil, and that history was fraught with ironies. The feudal and ecclesiastical arms engaged in a continuous medieval struggle to achieve absolute power, and the freedom that emerged was not the end striven for: the Roman empire contributed more to liberty than the republic did, Frederick the Great more to toleration than other, more enlightened, despots; without Peter the Great Europe might have been dominated by France and, but for Frederick William 1 of Prussia, by Russia. Appalling lapses and regressions into barbarism were always possible: the grotesque recrudescence of witchcraft and its persecution was not a product of the

Dark Ages but emerged 'in the bright dawn of our modern civilization'; it flourished during a revival of letters in the age of Shakespeare and Bacon, Racine and Bossuet, with divines, philosophers and statesmen vying with each other to promote it.[24] Random contingency played an enormous and unrecognized role: the errors of cartographers enabled Columbus to discover the new world; George I's hatred of his son led to the legitimization of Britain's two-party system as opponents of the King clustered around the Prince of Wales. Incalculable repercussions stemmed from chance occurrences: the sudden death of the Empress Elizabeth of Russia in 1762 spared Prussia from dismemberment and indirectly confirmed Britain's enormous colonial acquisitions in the treaty of Paris of the following year. That same treaty, having removed the threat of French troops in North America, initiated the colonies' movement towards independence. A 3d. duty imposed by Lord North on tea broke up Britain's mighty empire. A two-hour delay resulting from Louis XVI's gluttony at Étoges ruined the King's flight and entirely altered the course of the Revolution. Acton knew that the trivial was not always trivial, that seemingly irrelevant, minor facts made all the difference.

His overly optimistic view of future human advance was in part the consequence of his tendency to confuse progress in historical science with general progress. Since Bacon, Descartes, Pascal and Leibniz had insisted that the moderns were not inferior to the ancients, that the future did not mean an invariable declension from the golden age of the past, the world of ideas had made enormous advances, and Acton shared in this supreme intellectual confidence. History in particular had made staggering progress since 1815. A multitude of hypotheses were proposed and tested and either refuted or affirmed, and by this process an unassailable core of knowledge and interpretation was accumulated and stored. As a science its development was constant, inevitable and progressive; progressive both in its increased confidence and certitude and the wisdom it conferred, and in the way in which it freed the present from the shackles of the past with its recurring pattern of unenlightened prejudice and custom. History was 'the patrimony of mankind'; 'Without this, we move in a circle – the stone is always rolling back.' His *History of Freedom* was to conclude along the following lines: 'End: Reasons for Hope. Ignorance was at the bottom of it. This century has produced great securities. It strengthens and enlightens conscience. Discovered anthropology, statistics, political economy.'[25] Only in this limited sense was E.H.Carr right to accuse him of naive optimism and an unfounded liberal assumption that greater knowledge bestowed greater wisdom. Acton was shocked when Droysen suggested that for all the beauty of their poetry and sculpture the Greeks sighed for a tyrant like the Macedonians and feared freedom. He remained convinced of the omnipotence of ideas and especially certain that, in transforming and liberating, history must contribute to a juster society.

Acton's Prospectus for the *CMH* has encouraged the assumption that he believed in an absolutely objective and definitive history, a belief that G.N.Clark in his introduction to the *New CMH* decisively set out to destroy. But an element of boosterism along with the bright prospect of collaborative effort led him to overstate his case. Insofar as he thought of an ultimate history, it was as an ideal to be aimed for rather than an achievement to be accomplished in the present. His own generation's more modest task was to clear away the rubble of 'conventional mendacity' and collect documentary material in preparation for a fresh reappraisal. Like the coming of Christ's kingdom, ultimate history was an imperishable ideal by which to measure progress, and an awareness of the immensity of the task ahead is far more conspicuous in his writings than a sense of its accomplishments to date. Much had been done; far more remained. Studies which were considered classics a generation ago had lost their authority; all of Ranke's seventy works were being superseded; definitive histories were sparse islands dotted about a vast Pacific Ocean. In 1887 he told Döllinger that students were ignorant of the most essential problems of the French Revolution. In 1895, when delivering his lectures on the subject, he admitted that enigmas still proliferated; there was so little deciding evidence on so much detail; he could penetrate so far and no further. History would never possess the finished comprehensiveness, the satisfying formality of a Bradshaw or a Latin grammar. It was an object of ceaseless enquiry, 'a narrative told of ourselves, the record of a life which is our own, of efforts not yet abandoned to repose, of problems that still entangle the feet and vex the hearts of men'.[26]

Again, the accusation that Acton wrote disembodied, rarefied history is unfair, as anyone who has read the inordinately factual and conventional narrative form of his Cambridge lectures will confirm. If ideas were important it was because they were great propelling forces, positive and active. Thought preceded act, men fought and sacrificed their lives for ideals, however false or sullied by baser motives, and if at times Acton overstressed them it was because he thought they had been neglected by previous historians like Seeley who saw individual whigs but not whiggism as a principle. History was ethical not metaphysical, and action moved through the medium of right and wrong: 'No one has a true idea of right until he does it.'[27] The practical success of the American Revolution contributed far more to its French counterpart than did its revolutionary principles; the pre-revolutionary theories of Turgot and Rousseau were realized and enacted in specific legislation by the General Assembly. At the same time Acton never lost sight of the Parisian mob which cast its shadow over the deliberations at Versailles. While deputies talked of the cause, the people died for it, and their daemonic fury, their hunger and physical privations ultimately controlled the direction of the Revolution. His history found room for Columbus' geographical discoveries as well as Copernicus' new cosmology; he wrote on the balance of trade, not just the theology of predestination. Ideas were not abstractions, but were rooted in the soil of their time. Locke's contractual theorizing perfectly reflected the social and political status of the landed aristocracy of the seventeenth century. Nor was

Acton unaware of the complex impurities and balance of
forces which shaped laws; the Edict of Nantes was a recognition of Protestant power in France, not a principled concession
to tolerance. Similarly James II's seemingly liberal repeal of
the Test Act was conceived as a preliminary to absolutism.

His style, which is presumed to be cumbersome, diffuse
and pedantic, is, on the contrary, tight and trenchant and
epigrammatic. As his tendency to overquote, list authorities
and drop endless names grew, so his prose grew more powerful and concentrated. He could carry his learning lightly so
that in the midst of a dense discussion of Luther's Reformation
theology he relaxes and pictures Luther translating the New
Testament at Wartburg where he 'wore a moustache, dined
joyously, carried a sword, and shot a buck'. No military historian, he surmises as to why Dumouriez and his outnumbered
troops survived Valmy: 'The French stood their ground
because nobody attacked them, and they were not attacked
because they stood their ground.'[28] Far from being dry and
tedious, he was not always fastidious enough to curb the lurid
rhetorical sweep of his style or resist the splashing on of broad,
bright, primary colours. He confessed this artistry to his wife;
his wish to avoid surprises in developing his argument, pre-
paring the way by short, imperceptible steps, so that each
conclusion seemed inevitable and right. The young writer who
could argue persuasively for slavery in the United States could
equally deploy his later skill in urging a plausible but highly
misleading and one-sided interpretation of the American
Revolution.

On this principle of subversion [the American revolutionar-
ies] erected their commonwealth, and by its virtue lifted
the world out of its orbit and assigned a new course to
history. Here or nowhere we have the broken chain, the
rejected past, precedent and statute superseded by unwritten law, sons wiser than their fathers, ideas rooted in the
future, reason cutting as clean as Atropos.

Nor could he resist melodrama: 'Everybody knows how Monsieur Thiers, with 20,000£ in his hand and a loaded pistol in his pocket, met [Theiner] at midnight, in the loneliest alley of the Champs Élysées, and extorted his secret.' *Everybody?* And is this story true? He attempts to disarm and persuade with the aid of every cunning literary device. The insidious conjunction of adjectives in his essay on the St Bartholomew Massacre – 'holy deceit', 'pious dissimulation', 'cruel clemency', 'inhuman mercy' – subtly suggests moral disorientation and reinforces the central thesis of the Counter-Reformation's perversion of religious faith.[29] In private correspondence, especially, he rarely enters a qualifying clause and the unequivocal assertions harden into ruthless gems. His editors, Figgis and Laurence, asserted euphemistically that Acton was not prone to doubts; the more detached Henry Sidgwick observed that he threw off highly questionable assertions as if they were trite commonplaces. Readers of Acton should always beware and be on their guard.

The style was the man, and perhaps his critics were right to suggest that his Catholicism reinforced an already austere temperament. Creighton had questioned whether nineteenth-century tolerance was the result of Victorian virtue or the more practical consequence of a balance of parties which enforced a degree of mutual toleration. The ideal Christian state had encouraged the Inquisition's monstrous growth. 'The possession of a clear and definite ideal of society seems to me dangerous to its possessors.' Yet Acton held precisely to the ideal of a universal Church and a one-party state. There was an inevitable tension between Catholic and historian. The historian understood that 'heresy' was derived from the Greek 'hairesis' meaning choice, and that only later had it taken on its fateful pejorative meaning of false choice. He knew that the devout Mary Tudor burned and that the worldly Catherine de Medici tolerated. He conceded that a certain intolerance was inseparable from religion – if I am right you must be wrong, if my faith is true yours must be false –

and if truth was not absolute then liberty was a precondition for seeking a variety of truths. The historian appreciated that it was the breakaway sects, the Arminians and Quakers, who were the apostles of freedom, then secular philosophers like Franklin, Bentham and Mill who, more than any orthodox Christians, 'swept away that appalling edifice of intolerance, tyranny, cruelty, which believers in Christ built up, to perpetuate their belief'.[30] Now he found more to admire in the Protestant opinions of Rothe and Baur than in the utterances of the 500 bishops of the Vatican Council, and if the spirit of Gregory XIII continued to pervade the Church it were better that the work of destruction, initiated by Bismarck, Gambetta and Garibaldi, be completed. Towards the very end of his life he unequivocally supported the clash of ideals as against the ideal state, and confessed that only his impregnable Catholic faith divided him from Vinet's Protestant theology of conscience.

He leaves an uncertain legacy: an unobtainable ideal and a life and writings whose flaws exemplify its impossibility. But perhaps his sublime confidence is a worthwhile corrective to the more prevalent vanity of misguided humility. Acton's historical vocation was shaped from childhood. He possessed the necessary fascination and respect for facts and for details of the actual. Having seen a play as a child, he wrote to his mother asking whether the water which scalded Georgiana's fingers was really hot or sham. At Oscott he began a compendium of the chief facts in history, and from Munich he wrote to his stepfather justifying further studies under Döllinger: 'Judged by the standard of what constitutes an educated man, my studies were in great part superfluous and extraneous, and were appropriate only when looked upon in the light in which I viewed them... This was the unity of purpose; I did not study as a dilettante or a literary epicure. And if a common name is to be given to all these branches, I would call them historical.'[31] He possessed a highly developed sense of historical continuity and was intensely aware that the unseen past was always present and weighed down upon us.

He wished to reimagine and recreate that elusive but significant past, and its physical remains helped to evoke it: the
singed volume which Servetus carried with him to the stake
that Acton inspected in the Bibliothèque Nationale, the
yellowing plumes on Henry IV's armour which he saw in
the Venice arsenal, the almost perfectly preserved remains
of Tilly, the imperial commander during the Thirty Years'
War. He believed that a study of the past bestowed an extra
sense which enabled the historian, steeped in time and the
specific, to step outside it altogether. Why wait for posterity's
judgement on Mr Gladstone? Following an earlier conversation, Acton offered it at once: 'shut your eyes to my
handwriting,' he wrote to Mary Drew, 'and... you shall hear
the roll of the ages.'[32] By a strange alchemy a contemplation
of the unique and particular allowed the historian to escape
from the temporary and the transient, and to fasten on abiding
issues. History redeemed man from time.

Scholarship, knowledge, erudition were, by themselves,
inadequate, for the 'dust of archives blots out ideas'. Thinking
was better than learning, and the historian must reach for
more extended horizons, for higher levels of synthesis, beyond
the chronicle of fortunes and adventures, to grasp an underlying history that decisively shaped and moulded. The historian's task was to give meaning to history, to discern, through
vision and imagination, a causal pattern in what might
otherwise seem arbitrary and disconnected. It was this that
transformed history from 'a rope of sand', a 'burden on the
memory', into 'an illumination of the soul'. That illumination
derived, above all, from an interpretation of history as moral
drama, and Acton's reputation has suffered from this —
unfairly, because, far from usurping the historian's modest
role, it amounted, paradoxically, to a conscious acceptance
of the historian's limitations, an honest recognition that history was not a purely inductive science nor wholly objective.
And Acton's ethical framework had one further advantage,
in that it appreciated that man inhabited a moral universe,
that human beings were moral animals using an evaluative

language and who spoke and acted – rightly or wrongly – as if they were free, possessed the capacity to choose and were responsible for their actions and their consequences. He believed most passionately that mankind made their history and were not made by inexorable forces which irresponsibly exempted them. This gave the study of history its dignity. For just as each individual must make his life, so he must construct his inheritance, for 'knowledge of history means choice of ancestors'.[33]

Notes

ABBREVIATIONS

Acton

A–D: *Ignaz von Döllinger: Lord Acton Briefwechsel*, ed. Victor Conzemius (3 vols, Munich, 1963–71).

A–G: *Letters of Lord Acton to Mary, daughter of the Right Hon. W. E. Gladstone*, ed. Gerbert Paul (London 1904 and 1913: 1st edn quoted unless otherwise stated).

A–S: *The Correspondence of Lord Acton and Richard Simpson*, ed. Josef L. Altholz, Damian McElratha and James C. Holland (3 vols, Cambridge, 1971–75).

ECS: *Essays on Church and State*, ed. Douglas Woodruff (London, 1952).

EFP: *Essays on Freedom and Power*, ed. Gertrude Himmelfarb (London, 1956).

HES: *Historical Essays and Studies*, ed. J. N. Figgis and R. V. Laurence (London, 1907).

HOF: *The History of Freedom and Other Essays*, ed. J. N. Figgis and R. V. Laurance (London, 1907).

LFR: *Lectures on the French Revolution*, ed. J. N. Figgis and R. V. Laurence (London, 1910).

LMH: *Lectures on Modern History*, ed. J. N. Figgis and R. V. Laurence (London, 1906).

SC: *Selections from the Correspondence of the First Lord Acton*, ed. J. N. Figgis and R. V. Laurence (London, 1917).

SW: *Selected Writings of Lord Acton*, ed. J. Rufus Fears (Indianapolis, 1985), 2 cols to date.

Secondary Sources

Altholz: Josef L. Altholz, *The Liberal Catholic Movement in England* (London, 1962).

Fasnacht: G. E. Fasnacht, *Acton's Political Philosophy: An Analysis*

(London, 1952).

Himmelfarb: Gertrude Himmelfarb, *Lord Acton: A Study in Conscience and Politics* (Chicago, 1962).

Kochan: Lionel Kochan, *Acton on History* (London, 1954).

MacDougall: Hugh A. MacDougall, *The Acton–Newman Relations: The Dilemma of Christian Liberalism* (New York, 1962).

McElrath: Damian McElrath, *Lord Acton: The Decisive Decade 1864–74* (Louvain, 1970).

CHAPTER 1: THE REPUTATION

1. Edward Norman, *The English Catholic Church in the Nineteenth Century* (Oxford, 1984), p. 336. David Ogg, H. A. L. Fisher (London, 1947), p. 167. William H. McNeill, *Mythistory and Other Essays* (Chicago, 1986), p. 112. H. A. L. Fisher, *Studies in History and Politics* (Oxford, 1920), p. 93. Geoffrey Elton, 'Herbert Butterfield and the Study of History', *Historical Journal*, Vol. 27, No. 3, 1984, p. 732. A. J. P. Taylor, 'Diary', *London Review of Books*, Vol. 5, No. 9, p. 21.

2. *HOF*, p. 51.

3. *HES*, p. 488. Himmelfarb, p. 200.

4. *SC*, p. 308.

5. John Kenyon, 'The Historian as Hierophant', *The Times Literary Supplement*, 6 January 1978, p. 3. *Mary Gladstone (Mrs Drew) her Diaries and Letters*, ed. Lucy Masterman (London, 1930), p. 168. Owen Chadwick, *Acton and Gladstone* (London, 1976), p. 20. *A–G* (1913 edn), p. 189.

6. Chadwick, *Acton and Gladstone*, p. 18. *Mary Gladstone, Her Diaries and Letters*, p. 173. James Bryce, *Studies in Contemporary Biography* (London, 1911), p. 397.

7. H. Montgomery Hyde, *Henry James at Home* (London, 1969), p. 127.

8. *F. W. Maitland: Selected Papers*, ed H. A. L. Fisher (Cambridge, 1911), III, pp. 514–19.

9. Herman Finer, 'Acton as Historian and Political Scientist', *Journal of Politics*, Vol. 10, 1948, pp. 603–35. E. D. Watt, ' "Freedom" as an Incantation: The Example of Lord Acton', *Journal of Politics*, Vol. 25, 1963, pp. 461–71. The three seminal works were Friedrich Hayek's *The Road to Serfdom* (London, 1944),

Karl Popper's *The Open Society and Its Enemies* (2 vols, London, 1945) and Isaiah Berlin's *Historical Inevitability* (Oxford, 1954). Friedrich Hayek, *Studies in Philosophy, Politics and Economics* (London, 1967), p. 143. Robert L. Schuettinger, *Lord Acton: Historian of Liberty* (La Salle, 1976), p. 84.

10. *A–G*, p. 168.

11. Lytton Strachey, *Eminent Victorians* (Harmondsworth, 1948), p. 102.

12. E. H. Carr, *What Is History?* (Harmondsworth, 1961), p. 2. *LMH*, P. 12.

13. David Knowles quotes *King Lear* in *The Historian and Character* (Cambridge, 1963), p. 13. Herbert Butterfield, *The Whig Interpretation of History* (Harmondsworth, 1973), p. 80.

14. Herbert Butterfield, *Man on His Past* (Cambridge, 1969), p. 96. Brogan's remarks on Acton appeared in an appreciation of Herbert Butterfield published in *The Diversity of History* (Cambridge, 1970), ed. J. H. Elliott and H. G. Koenigsberger, pp. 2–4, 15. *Lord Acton: Lectures on Modern History* (London, 1960), p. 8.

15. Maurice Cowling, *Religion and Public Doctrine in Modern England* (Cambridge, 1980), I, p. xix.

16. 'Gasquet and the Acton–Simpson Correspondence', A. Watkin and Herbert Butterfield, *Cambridge Historical Journal*, Vol. 10, No. 1, 1950, pp. 75–105. For a brilliant discussion of Gasquet see Knowles, *The Historian and Character*, pp. 240–63.

CHAPTER 2: THE CATHOLIC

1. Edward Gibbon, *Autobiography* (Everyman edn, London, 1911), p. 12. *Gibbon's Journals*, ed. D. M. Low (London, 1929), pp. 122, 132.

2. Harold Acton, *The Bourbons of Naples, 1734–1825* (London, 1974), p. 185. See also Peter Gunn, *The Actons* (London, 1978).

3. David Mathew, *Lord Acton and His Times* (London, 1968), p. 35. *LMH*, p. 1.

4. *Letters and Diaries of John Henry Newman*, ed. J. S. Dessain and Thomas Gornall (Oxford, 1975), XXVII, p. 277. MacDougall, p. 128. *A–G*, p. 168.

5. *Acton Mss. Add. 5596*. Mrs H. Drew, 'Acton and Gladstone',

Fortnightly Review NS, 1 June 1918, p. 851.
6. Fasnacht, p. 198. Stephen J. Tonsor, *Victorian Studies*, December 1963, pp. 199–200.
7. *A–G*, p. 104.
8. *A–D*, III, p. 283. Stephen J. Tonsor, 'Lord Acton on Döllinger's Historical Theology', *Journal of the History of Ideas*, June–September 1959, p. 340.
9. *SC*, p. 2. E. S. Purcell, *The Life of Cardinal Manning* (London, 1895), II, p. 458.
10. Herbert Butterfield, 'Acton, His Training, Methods and Intellectual System', in A. O. Sarkissian (ed.), *Studies in Diplomatic History and Historiography* (London, 1961), p. 181, n. 48. *HES*, p. 342. Fasnacht, p. 46. *HES*, 342.
11. *HOF*, pp. 289, 292. 'Nationality' is also reprinted in *EFP*, pp. 141–70, and *SW*, I, pp. 409–33.
12. *HES*, p. 135. Sections of Acton's American Diary are printed in the *Fortnightly Review*, November and December 1921 (pp. 727–42, 917–34) and January 1922 (pp. 63–83), and *SW*, I, pp. 377–88. His 1861 essay on the Civil War is reprinted in *EFP*, pp. 171–224, *ECS*, pp. 291–338, and *SW*, I, pp. 216–62, and his 1866 reflections in *HES*, pp. 123–42, and *SW*, I, pp. 263–79.
13. *HOF*, p. 290. His 'Notes on the Present State of Austria' are reprinted in *ECS*, pp. 339–52. *LFR*, p. 115. *HOF*, p. 241. *A–S*, I. p. 149.
14. *SW*, II, p. 35.
15. *HOF*, p. 186. *ECS*, p. 394.
16. *HOF*, pp. 151–52.
17. *HOF*, p. 252. 'The Protestant Theory of Persecution' is reprinted in *HOF*, pp. 150–87, *EFP*, pp. 113–40, and *SW*, II, pp. 98–131, and 'Mr Goldwin Smith's Irish History' in *HOF*, pp. 232–69, and *SW*, II, pp. 67–97.
18. *HOF*, p. 562.
19. *A–D*, III, pp. 283–91. *HOF*, p. 410.

CHAPTER 3: THE LIBERAL CATHOLIC

1. *SC*, pp. 54, 56.
2. McRlrath, pp. 53–54.

3. *HES*, p. 283. *ECS*, pp. 38, 378.
4. *EFP*, p. 341. *SC*, p. 56.
5. *HOF*, pp. 31, 44.
6. *HOF*, p. 514. Himmelfarb, p. 44. Acton's case is powerful put in his 'Ultramontanism' of July 1863, reprinted in *ECS*, pp. 37–85.
7. Stephen J. Tonsor, 'Lord Acton on Döllinger's Historical Theology', *Journal of the History of Ideas*, June–September 1959, p. 351, n. 75.
8. *ECS*, p. 60. MacDougall, p. 127.
9. Matthias Buschkuhl, *Great Britain and the Holy See* (1982), p. 153. Herbert Butterfield, 'Journal of Lord Acton: Rome 1857', *Cambridge Historical Journal*, Vol. 8, No. 3, 1946, p. 193.
10. Mathew, *Lord Acton and His Times*, p. 70.
11. Purcell, *Life of Manning*, II, p. 323.
12. John Henry Newman, *Apologia Pro Vita Sua* (Everyman edn, New York, 1921), p. 221. Frederick J. Cwiekowski, *The English Bishops and the First Vatican Council* (Louvain, 1971), p. 51. Dessain and Gornall, *Letters and Diaries of Newman*, XXVII, p. 265.
13. *HOF*, p. 413. E. D. Watt, 'Rome and Lord Acton: A Reinterpretation', *Review of Politics*, October 1966, p. 495. *SC*, p. 59. Altholz, pp. 170–71. Kochan, p. 35, on whom the irony is also lost.
14. John Henry Newman, *An Essay on the Development of Christian Doctrine* (London, 1878), p. 3. MacDougall, pp. 157, 155. Altholz, p. 170.
15. MacDougall, pp. 175, 169.
16. Altholz, p. 166. Acton's journalism is given excellent coverage by both Altholz and MacDougall.
17. 'Notes on Archival Researches 1864–68', reprinted in McElrath, pp. 127–40.
18. McElrath, p. 53.
19. Both essays are reprinted in *ECS*, pp. 246–50, 251–59.
20. *HES*, p. 384. *A–S*, II, pp. 297–98. 'The Secret History of Charles II' is reprinted in *HES*, pp. 85–122, and *SW*, II, 132–62. David Ogg discusses the hoax in his *H. A. L. Fisher*, pp. 167–68, and Andrew Lang in 'The Master Hoaxer, James de la Cloche',

Fortnightly Review, September 1909, pp. 430–39.

21. The essay is reprinted in *HOF*, pp. 101–49, and *SW*, II, pp. 198–240. Acton's manuscript notes are quoted in Butterfield, 'Lord Acton and the Massacre of St Bartholomew', in *Man on His Past*, (p. 182, n. 1) on which I have relied heavily. Also Alfred Soman (ed.), *The Massacre of St Bartholomew* (The Hague, 1974), and N. M. Sutherland, *The Massacre of St Bartholomew and the European Conflict 1559–1572* (London, 1973).

22. *HOF*, pp. 123, 148. MacDougall, p. 27.

23. Buschkuhl, *Great Britain and the Holy See*, p. 162. *HOF*, p. 515. MacDougall, *Lord Acton on Papal Power* (London, 1973), p. 115.

24. *SC*, pp. 56, 91. *HOF*, p. 495.

25. *A–G*, Li.

26. McElrath, pp. 256, 261, 112–14. The four letters to *The Times* are reprinted in McElrath, pp. 246–61.

27. McElrath, p. 237. Newman's *Essay on Development*, p. 30. *Letters and Diaries of Newman*, ed. C.S.Dessain, XX, p. 224.

28. Victor Conzemius, 'Acton, Döllinger and Gladstone: A Strange Variety of Anti-infallibilists', in *Newman and Gladstone: Centennial Essays* (Dublin, 1978), ed. James D. Bastable, pp. 50–51. Gertrude Himmelfarb, *Victorian Minds* (London, 1968), pp. 164–65. E. D. Watt, 'Rome and Lord Acton: A Reinterpretation', *Review of Politics*, October 1966, pp. 503–04. Kochan, pp. 26–27.

29. Kochan, p. 24. My italics.

30. *SC*, p. 56.

CHAPTER 4: THE LIBERAL

1. *A–D*, III, pp. 257–72. Henry Scott Holland, *Personal Studies* (London, 1905), pp. 237–38. *A–G*, p. 174.

2. *A–G*, p. 105. *HOF*, p. xxxix.

3. Chadwick, *Acton and Gladstone*, p. 49.

4. J. J. Auchmuty, 'Acton: The Youthful Parliamentarian', *Australian and New Zealand Historical Studies*, May 1960, p. 138.

5. Acton to Gladstone, 23 August 1892, BM Add. Ms. 44094. The entire episode is well covered in Chadwick, *Acton and*

Gladstone, pp. 32–48.

6. Acton to Gladstone, 21 November 1868, BM Add. Ms. 44093. *A–G*, p. 199.

7. In a review of Thomas Erskine May's 'Constitutional History of England' *ECS*, p. 399. *A–G*, p. 49.

8. *HOF*, p. 79. Kochan, p. 91. *HOF*, p. 52.

9. Chadwick, *Acton and Gladstone*, p. 41, n. 1. *A–G* (1913 edn), p. 179. *HES*, p. 303.

10. Himmelfarb, p. 183. *HOF*, pp. 23, 11.

11. Himmelfarb, pp. 184, 185. Kochan, p. 134.

12. *HOF*, p. 23. *A–G*, pp. 90–92.

13. John Morley, *The Life of William Ewart Gladstone* (London, 1911), III, p. 131.

14. *ECS*, p. 451. Purcell, *Life of Manning*, II, p. 490.

15. Morley's *Life of Gladstone*, III, p. 343. And for Gladstone's repeated pleas for Acton to return home see Morley's *Life of Gladstone*, III, pp. 269, 271, 272.

16. *A–G* (1913 edn), pp. 176, 195. *SC*, pp. 207, 211.

17. *A–G*, pp. 45, 202.

18. *HOF*, p. 63. All three essays are reprinted in *HOF* and *SW*, I, and the first two in *EFP*.

19. *LFR*, p. 37. *HOF*, pp. 84, 21.

20. *HES*, p. 472. *A–G*, p. 99.

21. *A–G*, p. lxiv. *A–G* (1913 edn), p. 181. Himmelfarb, p. 175.

22. *A–G*, pp. 26, 212. Bryce to Acton, 30 April 1886, Acton Papers. George Watson, *Politics and Literature in Modern Britain* (London, 1977), p. 165.

23. *HOF*, p. 243.

24. *HOF*, p. 80.

25. Frederic Engel-Janosi, 'Reflections of Lord Acton on Historical Principles', *Catholic Historical Review*, 27, 1941, p. 177.

26. *LMH*, pp. 3, 4, 10, 11.

27. Kochan, p. 120. *HOF*, p. 278. Himmelfarb, *Victorian Minds*, p. 197.

28. *LMH*, p. 4. *LFR*, p. 351.

29. *HOF*, pp. 308, 585, 586.

30. *HOF*, pp. 579–80. Acton to Bryce, 25 March 1889, Ms. Bryce 1. Acton's review of Bryce is reprinted in *HOF*, pp. 575–87 and *SW*, I, pp. 395–405.

31. Kochan, p. 132. Himmelfarb, p. 219.

CHAPTER 5: THE HISTORIAN

1. BM Add. Ms. 44093. G. M. Trevelyan, *Clio: A Muse* (London, 1949), p. 183. *E. M. Forster's Commonplace Book*, ed. Philip Gardner (London, 1985), p. 159. I owe the *Sendschreiben* anecdote to Professor Owen Chadwick.
2. Acton Mss. Add. 8121. Doris S.Goldstein, 'The Origins and Early Years of The English Historical Review', *English Historical Review*, January 1986, p. 9.
3. ECS, pp. 431, 286–87. HES, p. 346. Newman's *Essay on Development*, p. 40.
4. HES, p. 389.
5. ECS, p. 288. HES, pp. 361, 360. Butterfield, *Man on His Past*, p. 12, n. 1.
6. A–G, p. 173. Butterfield, *Man on His Past*, p. 138, n. 1. HOF, p. 391. SC, p. 260.
7. ECS, p. 438. Butterfield, *Man on His Past*, p. 93.
8. LFR, p 92.
9. ECS, p. 404. SW, I, p. 156. LMH, p. 232.
10. HES, p. 426. Butterfield, *Man on His Past*, p. 87.
11. Kochan, p. 130. HES, p. 428. LMH, p. 26.
12. Sarkissian, p. 196. A–G, pp. 60–61.
13. A–S, I, p. 142. LMH, p. 318. ECS, p. 428.
14. Herbert Butterfield, *Lord Acton* (London, 1948), p. 12.
15. Kochan, p. 101. A–D, III, p. 288. LMH, p. 33. Himmelfarb, *Victorian Minds*, p. 179. Fasnacht, p. 39. HES, p. 437. EFP, p. 336.
16. Himmelfarb, pp. 217–18. LMH, p. 27.
17. St Matthew 5: v and viii. EFP, p. 339. HOF, p. 60.
18. Himmelfarb, p. 239. HES, p. 277.
19. EFP, p. 339. LFR, p. 373. LMH, p. 24. EFP, p. 335.
20. EFP, pp. 328–45.
21. LFR, p. 345. Sarkissian, p. 196. Butterfield, *History and Human Relations* (London, 1951), p. 118.
22. LMH, p. 109. LFR, 93, 300.
23. LFR, pp. 181, 239.
24. A–D, III, p. 439.
25. Fasnacht, pp. 203, n. 2, 244.
26. LMH, p. 8.
27. Fasnacht, p. 206.

28. *LMH*, p. 102. *LFR*, p. 218.
29. *HOF*, p. 586. McElrath, p. 133. *HOF*, pp. 112, 143.
30. *EFP*, p. 343. *SC*, p. 217.
31. *SC*, p. 24.
32. *A–G*, p. 50.
33. Butterfield, *Man on His Past*, p. 91. *LMH*, p. 317. Kochan, p. 135.

Index